CONSULATE GENERAL OF THE REPUBLIC OF LITHUANIA IN CHICAGO

Dear members and friends of the Waukegan-Lake County Lithuanian Community,

I would like to take this opportunity to extend my sincere appreciation to Dr. Robert Bakshis, the author of "Mes Lietuviai: A History of the Lithuanian-American Community of Waukegan-Lake County, Illinois".

Lithuanian history in Waukegan-Lake County stretches back to the 19th century. It was 1891 when the very first Lithuanians arrived in Waukegan and settled down. Since then, more and more Lithuanians started coming from Chicago and other areas, finding in Waukegan new opportunities, making it their home, and giving the base for the local Lithuanian community. Soon the community grew in numbers and activities, building a school, church and establishing St. Bartholomew's parish. Throughout the decades the Lithuanians kept its national spirit, expanded and built a number of facilities for the needs of the community, which later helped welcome displaced Lithuanians fleeing the occupation, and helping their brothers and sisters adapt and feel like home. As it has been for many decades, today the Lithuanian Community of Waukegan-Lake County is strong and active, preserving Lithuanian traditions, our culture, and making a positive impact on its members.

I am wholeheartedly grateful for the effort of everyone who helped make this community flourish, and particularly for the work of Dr. R. Bakshis, who has put together the wonderful story of the Lithuanians of Waukegan-Lake County, and for passing it on to the future generations.

Sincerely,

Mantvydas Bekešius
Consul General of the Republic of Lithuania in Chicago

CHAPTER BOARD

President
Gintautas Steponavicius
847-644-2871
upellis@sbcglobal.net
LAC Natl. Board Member

Exec. Vice President
Violeta Rutkauskiene
847-244-4943
LAC Natl. Board Member

Secretary
Jolita Vilimiene
847-975-0213
Midwest Dist. Bd. Member

Treasurer
Paulius Slavenas
847-405-0794
P. O. Box 363
Deerfield, IL 60015

Vice Presidents:

Palmira Januscniene-
Westholm
847-943-1046
LAC Natl. Board Member

Elena Skalisiene
847-541-3287

Vesta Steponaviciute
224-548-1646

Audit Committee:
Sigita Damasiene
Daiva Jasmanta
Ramute Kazlauskiene

**LAC National
Board Member**
Gediminas Damasius
847-362-8675

Annual Dues:
Adult $20
(age 18 and up)

**GEDIMINAS
LITHUANIAN CULTURAL
SATURDAY SCHOOL
Director**
Jurita Gionta
847-630-0098

LITHUANIAN AMERICAN COMMUNITY
(NOT-FOR-PROFIT CORPORATION)

WAUKEGAN-LAKE COUNTY CHAPTER

September 10, 2018

To:
**Robert Bakshis, Ed.D., Editor/Publicist of
"Mes Lietuviai": A History of the
Waukegan-Lake County, Illinois,
Lithuanian American Community (LAC)**

It must be noted that the most comprehensive project of Dr. Robert Bakshis has now become a treasure for the future generations who want to know about the Lithuanian American past and present residents in Waukegan and its surrounding communities. It can easily be seen that hour upon hour had to have been spent to glean the exhaustive information from various sources. We are most grateful for all of Dr. Bakshis efforts in this regard.

A similar project of our Waukegan-Lake County (W-LC) Chapter is materializing, and it is being prepared using the Lithuanian language rather than English. The scope of the project emphasizes the W-LC Chapter's activities from the time of the incorporation of LAC as a not-for-profit corporation, and aims to make a historical chronology and record of its past, present and future events.

Let us hope that in the relatively near future the W-LC Chapter will succeed in creating an internet archive where perhaps both of these projects would be accessible to all.

Sincerely,

Gintautas Steponavicius
W-LC Chapter President

Mes Lietuviai:
A History of the Waukegan-Lake County, Illinois Lithuanian American Community

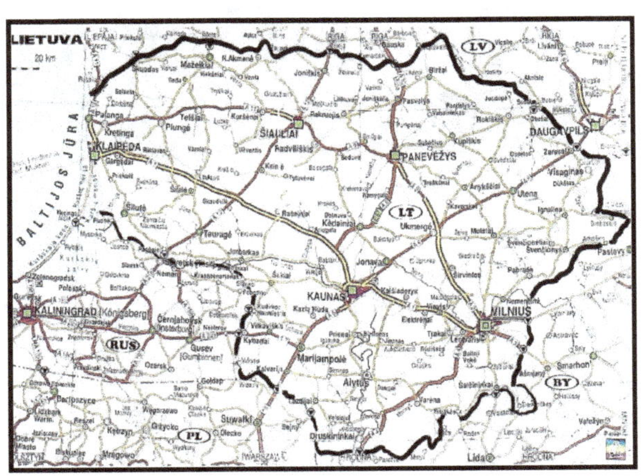

Robert Bakshis, Ed.D.

October 08, 1917

This book is dedicated to John and Sophie Bakshis

Cover Design by Elena Skalisius

Previous page Map of Lithuania adapted from "Lithuania at a Glance"
The Ministry of Foreign Affairs of the Republic of Lithuania 2007

ISBN 978-0-578-43714-9

Sisters of St. Casimir

2601 WEST MARQUETTE ROAD • CHICAGO, IL 60629-1817

(773) 776-1324 • www.ssc2601.com

September 1, 2018

Dear members and friends of the Waukegan-Lake County Lithuanian Community,

The Lithuanian Community in Waukegan and Saint Bartholomew's Parish and School in Waukegan have a unique connection with the beginnings of our congregation, the Sisters of St. Casimir, in Chicago. On September 20, 1912, just one year after our first Sisters came to Chicago, Venerable Maria Kaupas, our foundress, was asked to go to St. Bartholomew's to open and staff the school. Throughout the following seventy seven years, over 100 Sisters ministered in the parish and 14 young women became Sisters of St. Casimir, a testimony to the education these young women received and their desire to give back as Sisters of St. Casimir in service to those in need.

We are grateful for the opportunity to be part of the wonderful community of St. Bartholomew where we experienced the love and support of the people, shared their journey of faith and the love they had for their rich cultural heritage.

We congratulate Dr. Robert Bakshis on his publication of "Mes Lietuviai: A History of the Waukegan-Lake County, Illinois Lithuanian American Community."

May God bless you, all who are part of the Waukegan-Lake County Lithuanian Community, and all who will read and be inspired by this historical account of a people strong in their faith and love for their Lithuanian heritage.

Sister Regina Dubickas

General Superior
Sisters of St. Casimir

Dear friends,

This wonderful little history of the Lithuanian community and St. Bartholomew's parish would never have been written or handed down to future generations without the great work and efforts of Dr. Robert Bakshis to whom we all owe a debt of gratitude.

As you can see from this history the members of this parish community have, thru the years, contributed many good things to not only the city of Waukegan but the church of Chicago. Members of St. Bartholomew's have much to be proud of and this history of our religious community attests to the great spirit, energy, and enthusiasm of our Lithuanian ancestors and peers. I think those who read this will be most impressed by all that had been accomplished by those who gathered around the corner of 8th and Lincoln. I will be forever grateful that I had the privilege of pastoring my home parish for many years and hope that all those formed in faith in this community will feel the same.

"Didelius Aciu" to all our members for such great moments and memories. I am truly proud to be a Lithuanian American and grateful to all the folks who helped and formed me thru the years.

Fr. Bill Zavaski

Fr. Bill Zavaski

St. Bartholomew Class of 1957
Pastor of St. Bartholomew Church 1979-1991

Table of Contents

Birds around lighthouse are the Lithuanians who flew over the ocean to the USA.
The Birds are the colors of the Lithuania flag.
The fog cutter symbolizes Waukegan or shores of Lake County.
On the lighthouse the letters 'W L C A' – stand for 'Waukegan Lake County Apylinke'

Picture by Elena Skalisius

Preface

Marcus Lee Hansen proposed in a 1938 essay what has come to be known as "the third generation hypothesis." Simply stated "What the son wishes to forget the grandson wishes to remember".[1] Immigrants would bring to this country their language, culture and religion. Their primary goal was to become Americans, live a good life and provide for their children's future. When an immigrant arrived in the United States they could live in their own ethnic enclaves and live out their lives without becoming absorbed into their new society. Their children, however, wanted to blend in to American culture and often tried to distance themselves from their heritage. They avoided speaking their parent's native language when outside of the home, and tried to blend in to their environment to the best of their abilities.

Anecdotal family stories support Hanson's hypothesis:

Dad laughed and said he remembered some 10-12 year-old kids giving his dad a hard time about being an immigrant. They would come into the store and tease grandpa. He'd then chase them out of the store. They came back several times, and said he could never catch them. With that challenge he chased them all over the neighborhood and down the alleys with his belt. I guess he did catch up with a few of them and gave them a few swats.

---

[1] Marcus Lee Hansen. The Problem of the Third Generation Immigrant. Rock Island, Ill.: Augustana Historical Society, 1938, p.9.

Another time one of the kids called grandpa a foreigner. Grandpa asked him how long he had lived in the US. The kid said "10 years." Grandpa told him that he had lived in the US for over 20 years. So he was more of an American than the kid.[2]

Often children of immigrants would feel stigmatized by their ethnicity and tried to distance themselves from their parent's culture. They did not want to be different from the general American culture. They would learn their parent's language, but would not make a concerted effort to pass the language to the next generation. Likewise cultural traditions were abandoned or ignored to the point where the ethnic identity of the immigrant's grandchildren was muted.

The grandchildren of the immigrants were the third generation. Hansen believed that they would have a renewed interest in their cultural heritage and attempt to recapture the traditions and culture of their ancestors. Their interest would be made difficult because of their lack of skill with their ancestor's language.
Ethnicity and religion are highly correlated. The first census in independent Lithuania, in 1923, reported: Catholic — 85.7 percent; Jewish — 7.7 percent; Protestant — 3.8 percent; Greek Orthodox — 2.7 percent.[3] In Waukegan the Lithuanian community developed around St. Bartholomew Catholic Church on the south side of Waukegan.

---

[2] Conversation with John Bakshis, 2002
[3] Vytautas Vaitiekūnas "Lithuania", Assembly of Captive European Nations, 1965

St. Bartholomew was one of the 12 apostles of Jesus Christ. After the resurrection Bartholomew is said to have evangelized in India and Armenia.

> The manner of his death, said to have occurred at Albanopolis in Armenia, is equally uncertain; according to some, he was beheaded, according to others, flayed alive and crucified, head downward, by order of Astyages, for having converted his brother, Polymius, King of Armenia. On account of this latter legend, he is often represented in art (e.g. in Michelangelo's Last Judgement) as flayed and holding in his hand his own skin. His relics are thought by some to be preserved in the church of St. Bartholomew-in-the-Island, at Rome. His feast is celebrated on 24 August.[4]

St. Bartholomew Church was a "national church" and had no set boundaries for the parish. But the Lithuanian community occupied roughly the area between Cummings Street on the north, 10th Street on the south, McAllister Street on the east and Commonwealth Avenue on the west. There were additional parishioners from neighboring North Chicago and Lake County. Today the community is dispersed throughout Lake, McHenry

---

[4] Catholic Encyclopedia: St. Bartholomew –
   http://www.newadvent.org/cathen/0213c.htm

and northern Cook County. St. Bartholomew's parish has been closed and is no longer the focal point of their activities.

For Waukegan's Lithuanians almost seven generations have come and gone. The memories of early founders of the Waukegan Lithuanian community are fading rapidly. This book is intended to capture some of these memories so that future generations can appreciate their history. Topics of discussion will include the three waves of immigration: early economic immigrants, post-WWII displaced persons, and the Lithuanian American Community that developed after Lithuanian independence from the Soviet Union in 1990. While these three waves of immigrants share a common language and heritage, each occupy a unique place in history. Other topics of discussion are businesses, notable personalities, military service, civic organizations, and traditions.

Early Immigrants

Lithuanian immigrants have been coming to America since the very early days of European settlement. The incentives for relocation remained constant over time. Poor economic conditions in the old country coupled with the hope for a better future for themselves and their families provided the encouragement to leave the known world for the unknown.

The first documented Lithuanian in America was Alexander Carolus-Curšius. He served as the first schoolmaster of a Latin school in New Amsterdam from 1659 to 1661. For the next 200 years there was just a trickle of immigrants from Lithuania.

Leaving one's homeland is not done on a whim. Serious thought has to be given to leaving behind family, friends and the known. That decision is not easy. Generally people do not relocate unless there is a poor situation at home coupled with expectations for a better life somewhere else. Lithuania under the Russians was a feudal society until serfdom was abolished in Lithuania in 1861. An unsuccessful uprising against Russian rule in January 1864 led to the Russians imposing repressive measures against the Lithuanians. There was an attempt at Russification of the country. The plan included the banning the use of the Lithuanian language in school, commerce, and business. The bans continued until the Russian Revolution in 1905.

After a famine in Lithuania, large numbers of Lithuanians immigrated to the United States between 1867 and 1868. These immigrants were attracted by economic growth in America's industrial areas. Between 1868 and 1914, approximately 635,000 people, almost 20 percent of the population, left Lithuania. Lithuanian cities and towns were growing under the Russian rule, but the country remained underdeveloped by European standards. Living conditions were difficult and job opportunities were limited.

In an interview with the author, Anna Zemaitis-Bakshis-Chapas (1903-1999), described life in rural Lithuania prior to her immigration in 1920 from Girkalnis, Lithuania:

> When I came here to America my heels were all black and cracked for a year's time. I used to walk bare foot all the time.
>
> One time someone invited me to be a bride's maid. I didn't have any shoes, so I borrowed my mother's shoes. They were so big. They were high tops, I walked Womp! Womp! Womp! Womp!   No one even wanted to even dance with me. I borrowed a gray skirt, black belt and white shirt. I guess the shirt was mine.   I was dressed beautiful, but mother's shoes! Ah yes Maria, I don't want to go to Europe any more. If someone take me, I walk back again - right across the ocean.
>
> I don't wanta at all. The way I live, in the fall it was dark, muddy, and go barefooted at nighttime and feed those pigs and milk the cows. And early in the morning you had to go with the cows to the

field.   Kids wanta sleep not to get up in the morning. Before sunrise we go until later. Just go to sleep and you had to get up already.   In the night time we had to go watch the horses, they only eat in the night time. In the daytime they are working. Bring them water, two buckets.

All over other countries work too. That is why they all want to get in here.

Look in the French.   They live in this room peoples, live in another room cows under one roof - animals and people. We have nice home and everything. My father bought them, but have a lots of mortgage. But my father liked to parties and everything and we didn't have clothes - nothing. And he worked Jesus, Mary in the summer time he go into the oats and the rice and the everything to clean them up and father goes to plant the seeds. He planted the seeds and we had to go and mark it with the foot where the seeds fall so he go from there to there. Dig the potatoes on our knees. They plow a row of potatoes with the horses and then we go on our knees and pick up the potatoes.

I don't even want to think about Europe and how I live. My sister was down town she dressed up with shoes. In the winter time my father would make soles out of wood and some skin, and that is how

we would walk with wooden shoes. In the summer
time Momma gave us the shoes *(Momma = mother
nature; therefore = barefoot)*.[5]

Immigrants saw America as a place where they could build a better life for themselves and their families. They first headed to new industrialized jobs in Massachusetts and the coal mines of Pennsylvania. Some viewed America as a place to earn their fortunes and then return to their homeland; while others became permanent citizens of the United States. Work conditions were often dangerous, work hours were long, and the jobs offered little pay. Yet life in America offered more hope than life in Lithuania. Upton Sinclair's 1906 groundbreaking novel <u>The Jungle</u> describes the life

of Jurgis Rudkus, a Lithuanian immigrant, who worked in the meatpacking houses of Chicago in the early 1900's. Sinclair described working conditions where owners of factories took advantage of their workers. Company towns were built where rent, food, and drink were controlled by the company. At the end of a pay period a workers expenses were often equal to or greater than their income. Sinclair described an environment where immigrant's lack of language skills and "modern" society set them up to be victims of unscrupulous financiers and business men. For Sinclair, labor union membership was seen as the path to better living conditions.

Drawn by jobs, Lithuanians came to the United States, entering through Ellis Island in New York, and through the Port of

---

[5] Robert Bakshis conversation with Anna Zemaitis-Bakshis-Chapas, November 29, 1975.

Baltimore. The story of John and James Bakshis is typical of many immigrants:

> John and James Bakshis were with their parents in Lithuania until the death of their father. They were unable to keep up the farm and decided to come to the United States. Jim came in 1911, about the age of 14. John was not allowed to come at that time because of "pink eye". He came a year later. They had to leave during the night to get across the border. The border guards would be paid by the person who was helping to get people out of the country. Once in Germany they were free to travel how and where they pleased. John was 21 years old when he came – the mother was left in Lithuania. Three older brothers were already in the States. Several years after James arrived in the U.S. he had trouble with a bone disease which caused his back to "hunch". He had a very sharp mind for figures and business and eventually opened a grocery and meat market with his brother John at 1002 8th Street, Waukegan, IL.[6]

John left Germany through the port of Bremen, German. According to his naturalization papers he had booked passage on the North German Lloyd Line ship Main. The Main could carry

---

[6] Eva Bakshis conversation with Anna Zemaitis-Bakshis-Chapas, Winter 1985.

369-2nd, 217 3rd, and 2,865-4th class passengers. He arrived in America on June 20, 1912, entering through the Port of Baltimore

From their port of entry Lithuanian immigrants migrated to mining and industrial centers in the East and Midwest. In Illinois, Lithuanian communities were established in the cities of Chicago, Rockford, Springfield, Bellville, Spring Valley, and other locations. In 1891 the Washburn & Moen Company built a steel wire mill on Waukegan's lakefront for the purpose of manufacturing iron and copper wire nails and barbed wire. The company purchased a very large parcel of land for its complex. Part of the parcel was used for the factory and the remainder of the property was for a company town to house employees. North of 10th Street the company town eventually became part of Waukegan and south of 10th street became North Chicago.

Other manufacturers in Waukegan were Chicago Hardware Foundry Co. (grey iron castings and light machinery), Atwater Manufacturing Co. (revolving signs), Chicago Hardware Co. (locks and builders' hardware), Pfanstiehl Electric Laboratory (induction coils and electrical apparatus), North Chicago Forge Co. (portable forges), North Chicago Machine Co. (carburetors), Louisville Vulcan Smelting Co. (zinc, brass, lead and by-products), Chicago Cement Block Machine Co. (cement block machines), Metallic Reproduction Co. (jewelry), Great Lakes Manufacturing Co. (notary public and other seals), North Chicago Tool Co. (emery wheels), National Envelope Co. (envelopes and cards of all descriptions), Republic Fence & Gate Co. (wire fencing and ornamental gates), Practical Gas Engine Co. (engines), U.S. Sugar Refinery, Wilder Tanning Co., Alshuler's

Garment Factory and the Thomas Brass and Iron Works.[7] Together, these manufacturers offered many opportunities for unskilled immigrant labor. In 1900 the population of Waukegan was 4,915.

The first Lithuanian in Waukegan was drawn by the jobs provided by these factories.

> In 1891 Domininkas Norkevičia-Norkus came to Waukegan from Chicago on foot. He was the only Lithuanian in Waukegan. On November 1, 1891 the Washburn and Moen Co moved to Waukegan bringing many workers along with it, among them Mataušas Rūta and Antanas Jesiukevičius. Domininkas Norkus met them the next day and that made three Lithuanians in Waukegan. They used to earn eight dollars a week. Today there are workers who earn not eight, but fifteen dollars a day.[8]
>
> Eventually they all had families. Mataušas Rūta had thirteen children. Two died, while eleven grew up. Later they were joined by Jonas Visockis who

---

[7] Slayer, Carl. "The City of North Chicago" in John J. Halsey - A History of Lake County, Illinois. Harmegnies and Howell, Chicago, IL. 1912 p. 780

[8] To earn $8 per week at about thirteen cents per hour a worker would need to put in a 60 hour week. That would be 5 12-hour days. In terms of value adjusted for inflation through 2018 the Company initially paid them $205 per week, and in 1946 they earned $207 per week - or $5 per hour for a 40 hour week.

also came to Waukegan. He was sort of a businessman; he ran a boardinghouse. The following year they were joined by Kazys Gustas, Kazys Vaitekūnas and Vincas Zupkus.[9]

As the Lithuanian population grew the immigrants quickly began to organize. On December 9, 1894 the St. Bartholomew Men's Society was incorporated by the State of Illinois as a benevolent society. The first officers of the St. Bartholomew Society were: President, Kazimieras Vaitekūnas; Vice President Vincentas Zupkus; Secretary, Juozapas Bravinskas; Financial Recorder Mikolas Miklesevičius; and Treasurer Pranas Jocius, Assistant Treasurers Mataušas Rūta and Domininkas Norkus, Marshals Juozas Paleckis and Povilas Kaulius. Among the members of the society were Simon Kacuzis, Peter Wembris, Bartholomew Baresa, Matthew Valentikonis, John Jakutis, Jacob Janasauskas, Vincent Kairaitis, John Vaitekūnas, John Paulauskas, Felix Druba, Justin Juncer and Joseph Moncinskas.[10]

---

[9] Juozis Čužaukas, Nusekę Antplūdžiai Waukegan'o Lietuvių Istorija, page 4
[10] Svento Baltramiejaus Draugija 50 Auksinis Jubiliejus, page 3

Kazimieras (Charles) Vaitekūnas
St. Bartholomew's Society - First President

Washburn and Moen supplied housing for their new employees. The original dormitory building located on the southeast corner of 8th Street and Prescott. A few years later this building and land was donated to the Catholic Church. In keeping with the frugal nature of immigrants the two story boarding house was moved to 8th and Lincoln using horses and manpower. The building was repurposed as a church and school.

A history of the parish states:

> The first church property was donated by the Washburn and Moen company (of Worcester, Mass) to Poles and Lithuanians of Waukegan. The old frame house (at 8th St and Lincoln Ave) was converted into a church for both nationalities. With the influx of Lithuanian pioneers, however,

they took possession of the common church property.[11]

By 1900 the population of Waukegan had risen to 9,426 and North Chicago hosted an additional 1,150. St. Bartholomew's parish was organized on the Feast day of St. Bartholomew, August 24, 1896. This date was the first of two dates to be celebrated annually by the parish. The first infant to be baptized at St. Bartholomew's was Michael E. Gust on December 6th 1896.

Initially, St. Bartholomew Church was a mission church of St. George's Parish in Chicago. St. George's Parish was the first Lithuanian parish in the Chicago Archdiocese and St. Bartholomew's was the second. The Rev. Matthew Kraučunas celebrated the mass twice a month until 1900 when Fr. Edward Stefanowicz (Steponavičius) an assistant at St. George in Chicago was named the first pastor. He was replaced in 1901 by Fr. Matthew Smolenskas, who was the first full-time pastor of the parish. A parish school was organized and opened in with 30 children in 1901.

---

[11] The New World of October 25, 1946

St. Bartholomew School and Church
Circa 1908

When Fr. Smolenskas passed away in 1904, at the age of 44, there was a void in the parish that led to some conflict.

> In our parish the fight is on again. When the Rev. Smolenskas died the parishioners appealed to the archbishop for a priest. The archbishop replied that six priests are coming from Lithuania. He will send one of the priests to the Waukegan parish. As they were waiting for the priest from Lithuania, the priest Ambrozaitis arrived. He said that he came from Chicago. On the next day the priest left the parish. The parishioners were very much discouraged. On the next day the priest's maid came and demanded the keys of the rectory. The parishioners refused to give the key and refused to permit her to occupy the rectory. The maid broke

into the rectory by force. The next day the priest
Ambrozaitis arrived. At once the priest demanded
that the rectory be decorated and that electric lights
should be installed.

On the 1st of May Rev. Abrozaitis held a parish
meeting. He did not care to ask the parishioners if
they accepted him or not, but at once demanded the
collection, etc.[12]

The conflict persisted. About six weeks later a letter appeared in
the newspaper Lietuva:

After the death of the priest Smolenskas now we
have the Rev. Ambrozaitis as rector. The harmony
between the parishioners and the rector did not last
long. The first struggle came over the collection of
money. There are two collections, one for the seats
and the other the collection of cents. With the Rev.
Smolenskas the parish had both collections under its
control; now Rev. Ambrozaitis has tried to take both
collections under his control, but the parish
committee refused. Then the priest demanded the
cents collection, and besides that collection he
demanded various improvements to the rectory . . .[13]

Fr. Ambrozaitis was in charge of only one year. According to the
1906 Catholic Directory, St. Bartholomew Church had no pastor

[12] Lietuva, Vol. XII, No. 21, May 20, 1904
[13] Lietuva, July 8, 1904

for 1905. It was being "attended from the Polish church of Holy Rosary, North Chicago."[14] Finally, from 1906-1909 Fr. Joseph Stočkus assumed the position of pastor.

In 1909 Fr. Michael Krušas became pastor. Under the direction of Fr. Krušas the original dormitory building at 914 8th Street was bulldozed and a school was built on the site at a cost of $17,000.

St. Bartholomew Church and School
Circa 1912

On September 20, 1912 The Sisters of St. Casimir began their teaching ministry in Waukegan. They began with 275 students in four classroom teaching grades 1 through 6. They continued their service until May 31, 1989.

The Sisters of St. Casimir (the patron saint of Lithuania) were a new order that was dedicated to the support and education of the Lithuanian community of the United States. Bishop John

---

[14] A History of the Parishes of the Archdiocese of Chicago, 1980. Volume II, Page 1587

Shanahan, Bishop of Harrisburg, PA on August 28, 1907 said to first three novitiates: "You will be called Sisters of St. Casimir."[15] The next day the three women: Casimira Kaupas, Judith Dvaranauskas and Antania Unguraitis received the white veils of novices the next day. Hence August 29th would be commemorated a "Founding Day" for the Sisters of St. Casimir. The sisters completed their religious training under the guidance of the Sisters of the Immaculate Heart of Mary in Scranton, PA. The Sisters of the Immaculate Heart of Mary also provided administrative services for the new order for the first couple of years until they were able to operate by themselves. By 1911 there were 17 sisters in the order, and by 2012 their numbers had increased to 476. Over 130 Sisters of St. Casimir taught at St. Bartholomew's.

Mother Maria Kaupas, Mother M. Immaculata Dvaranauskas and
Mother M. Concepta Unguraitis

The first school to be staffed by the Sisters of St. Casimir was Holy Cross School in Mt. Carmel, PA. (1908). All Saints School

---

[15] Sisters of St. Casimir – A Journey in Faith – 100 Years 1907-2007; Booklink, Ireland copyright 2007 page 14

in the Roseland neighborhood of Chicago followed in 1911. In 1912 St. Bartholomew's School in Waukegan and St. Casimir School in Philadelphia were added. Thus St. Bartholomew School became the second grammar school in the Chicago Archdiocese, and the third in America, to be staffed by members of the Sisters of St. Casimir. The school was staffed by four Sisters of St. Casimir. Mother Maria Kaupas taught at St. Bartholomew's serving as the first Superior of St. Bartholomew's from September 1912 until August 24, 1913. She served with Sr. M. Kazimiera, Sr. M. Natalija and Sr. M. Bonaventura.

Mother Maria Kaupas was then elected the first Mother General of the new Congregation. She served as Mother General until her death April 17, 1940. Efforts are now underway advocating her canonization to sainthood.

It wasn't until 1919 that St. Bartholomew school was able to have a graduation class. This class had seven members: five boys and two girls.

1919 – St. Bartholomew Grade School – 1969
First Graduation Class

Among the groups hosted by St. Bartholomew's parish was the LRKSA (Lietuvių Romos Katalikų Susivienijimas Amerikoje – Lithuanian Roman Catholic Alliance of America). The group served a variety of purposes. The group supported Lithuanian nationalism, St. Bartholomew's parish, and also was viewed as a labor union that supported a socialist agenda. Undoubtedly the union was an active participant in the violent September 1919 strike against U.S. Steel and Wire (formerly Washburn and Moen) that required intervention by the state militia.

Following WWI, Lithuanian independence was reestablished. February 16, 1918 became known as Lithuanian Independence Day. This date was the second date to be celebrated annually by the community.

Immigration from Lithuania to the United States continued until about 1915 when Germany occupied Lithuania at the start of WWI. Following the war, anti-immigrant, nativist forces in the

U.S. Congress passed two laws that severely limited immigration. The Emergency Quota Act of 1921 limited immigration from any country to 3% of the number of persons from that country who were living in the U.S. as counted in the Census of 1910. Three years later restrictions were increased when the Immigration Act of 1924 further reduced immigration by setting the limit at 2% of the number of people from a given county already living in the United States as of the 1890 census.[16] Given that immigration from Eastern Europe was just getting started in 1890 the laws effectively excluded immigration for eastern and southern Europe. In addition, and Lithuanians were often mislabeled as "Polish" or "Russian." In 1928 the quota for immigration from Lithuania was set at 344 per year. These actions by the United States coupled with German and Russian occupation of Lithuania, effectively stopped immigration from Lithuania to the United States until after WWII when displaced persons were allowed entry. However, the immigration quota system remained in place until the Immigration and Nationality Act of 1965 was passed and restrictions were modified.

The 1920 census set the population of Waukegan at 19,226 and North Chicago at 5,839. The St. Bartholomew school enrollment in 1921 was 305 children. A conservative estimate would be that the Lithuanian community was about 10% of Waukegan's population.

---

[16] Immigration Act of 1924 – Wikipedia
    https://en.wikipedia.org/wiki/Immigration_Act_of_1924

1922   American Steel and Wire Mill   1927

The community celebrated its Lithuanian heritage and St. Bartholomew by holding annual celebrations in August. These were large affairs featuring picnics, parades, and parties. These celebrations continue to the present day with sponsorship by the Lithuanian American Community of Lake County.

Over the next couple of decades pastors came and went. In 1931 Fr. Joseph Čužauskas was assigned as pastor. He served as pastor from 1931 until his death at age 68 in 1955.

On Saturday evening July 22, 1933 at 5:30 p.m. fire swept St. Bartholomew's Church. Fr. Čužauskas and a few men from the parish managed to save the sacraments and move them to a room in the school.

In the history narrative written by Fr. Čužauskas in 1946 he hints that the fire was arson:

> We have plenty of brave people in our parish. Everybody with a small spark is trying to scare the pastor soon you will see, that the parish made the fire and is trying to burn the pastor. Who made the fire is trying to explain themselves that they never thought that from a small spark they would make a huge fire. They planned to just scare him. In the meantime they damaged the priest's health and honor that they would never bring back together.[17]

On Sunday morning, without a church, mass was held in the school. Four classrooms were still too small to accommodate everyone. By the next Sunday men had connected two classrooms. While this was better, those parishioners in the other rooms had difficulty following the mass. A request was made to the archdiocese for an additional priest so that mass could be celebrated concurrently in different rooms. At first a priest was sent to help on Sundays but he did not speak Lithuanian. Eventually a newly ordained priest, Fr. Walter Urba, was permanently assigned to the parish.

The parish embarked on an ambitious program to build a new church and pay off all the parish debt.

---

[17] Juozis Čužaukas, Nusekę Antplūdžiai Waukegan'o Lietuvių Istorija, page 14.

For 34 years the school had gone without repairs.
It was initially thought that his could be taken care
of with a few thousand dollars. Architects checked
the school and determined that the repairs would
cost $27,000. Members thought the cost was high
for both, yet we needed to repair the school. Now
we are bolder – we worked hard and gained
experience at this work.

The old parish debt of $34,000 was paid off. The new church
construction cost was $73,000. School repairs were $24,000. The
total cost was $131,000.[18]

Fr. Čužauskas came to be known known as a persistent fundraiser.
When he visited the homes of prospective donators Fr. Čužauskas
would ask for money directly asking: "Duok man šimtą" ("Give
me a hundred"). This was substantial sum of money in
depression-era 1933, and required great sacrifice; yet the
parishioners dug deep into their pockets and provided the funds to
build a new church. Fr. Čužauskas' pitch would go like this:

> "What do you think of the new church?" That's
> how he used to ask everyone when he would walk
> in.

> When he received the answer "YES", he would
> explain:

> You can't build the church without bricks, without
> workers; you need money. If five hundred

---

[18] Juozis Čužaukas, Nusekę Antplūdžiai Waukegan'o Lietuvių Istorija, page 6.

parishioners would give each a one hundred dollar bill, that would add up to $50,000 for the new church. Committing to pay a quarter per week, through eight years you would be able to pay $100 for the new church building; half a dollar per week, it would take four years to pay a hundred dollars; paying one dollar per week would take two years; paying two dollars per week, pay on hundred dollar per year.[19]

The parish foundation program received contributions from 277 families that totaled $28,087. Contributions ranged from $100 to $856. The average contribution was $137 and the median contribution was $115. In 2017 dollars this would be the equivalent of $520,734 total with an average contribution of $1,080, and a median contribution of $907 for each family.

June 14, 1936
St. Bartholomew Graduation

Top: Richard Rayunas, Leonard Stanulis, Stanley Leonitis, Albert Dagis, John Jarusis, Adolph Juncer.

Middle: Alex Kapter, John Bakshis, Bernice Rachius, Anna Galinis, Lucy Tauchius, John Novak, Adolph Kapter.

Front Alphonse Zaborski, Stanley Urban, Fr. Joseph Čužauskas, Fr. Walter Urba, Leonard Leonitis, Albin Ludas.

St. Bartholomew Graduation Class - June 14, 1936

---

[19] Juozis Čužaukas, Nusekę Antplūdžiai Waukegan'o Lietuvių Istorija, page 16.

On September 11, 1938 the new church was dedicated.

The church is a modern gothic style. It seats 450 people – 50 in the gallery. So the total that can be seated in the church is 500 people.
The church has three altars. The great altar is of white marble, brought from Italy. It was dedicated by Bishop J.E. O'Brien.

The church has stained glass windows. The lattice is made of marble. The benches are of gothic oak.

The church has two confessionals. The lighting is the best.

At the front of the church there is a statue of St. Bartholomew.[20]

New Church Dedicated September 1938

---

[20] Juozis Čužaukas, Nusekę Antplūdžiai Waukegan'o Lietuvių Istorija, page 6.

Traditionally on Christmas eve-day families would clean the front steps to their apartments so that Fr. Čužauskas could come for his annual visit. Fr. Čužauskas would visit as many families as he could to bless the food, distribute plokštelė and collect personal Christmas donations.

Midnight mass was virtually required. On most evenings kids would be in bed by 9 o'clock. But on Christmas Eve all the children of the parish assembled in their classrooms and were marched into church in one large procession. All the altar boys of the parish had to wear their acolyte robes and march with the priests.[21]

Confirmation Class

3rd and 4th Grade Classes

St. Bartholomew's 1940

Lithuania existed as an independent country until June 1940. The secret Molotov–Ribbentrop Pact between Germany and Russia (August 23, 1939) divided Eastern Europe into German and Russian spheres of influence. The pact set the stage for Germany's invasion of Poland (September 1, 1939) and the

---

[21] John Bakshis conversation with Robert Bakshis, December 2001

annexation of Lithuania by the Soviet Union (June 1940). The occupation of Lithuanian by the Russians was followed by mass arrests and deportations with Lithuania having 34,000 citizens removed. According to a Lithuanian government official, this was the start of a planned removal of 700,000 from Lithuania. This forced annexation was never recognized by the United States. The takeover of Lithuania by Russia gave new focus to groups within the United States to work for the re-establishment of a free and independent Lithuanian state.

1938 Lithuanian Lovers of Liberty – Waukegan Chapter

Lovers of Liberty Pin [22]
Circa 1911

---

[22] "D.L.L. Myletojų" = "Draugija Lietuvos Laisvės Myletojų" = "Lovers of Lithuanian Liberty"

Following the war, retuning GIs married and established new families starting what is known as the Baby Boom (1946-1964). Sufficient housing for the GIs and their new families was not available in the "old neighborhood" so they began to disperse throughout Waukegan, North Chicago and elsewhere in Lake County. However, St. Bartholomew's, being a national parish without boundaries, remained the focal point for many.

The St. Bartholomew Society celebrated its 50th jubilee in May 1945 with a gala affair at the Lithuanian Hall. The society had been instrumental in the formation of the parish and had worked tirelessly for the benefit of the community. St. Bartholomew Parish celebrated its 50th anniversary in 1946. Fr. Čužauskas prepared a book containing a history of the parish, a detailed review of the parish finances, and a collection of his homilies.

In 1946 there were 130 students in the school. Tuition for the students was as follows: for one child the fee is $1 per month; for two – 75 cents; for three 50 cents. The school is in nine grades and is in session for ten months.[23]

---

[23] Juozis Čužaukas, Nusekę Antplūdžiai Waukegan'o Lietuvių Istorija, page 6.

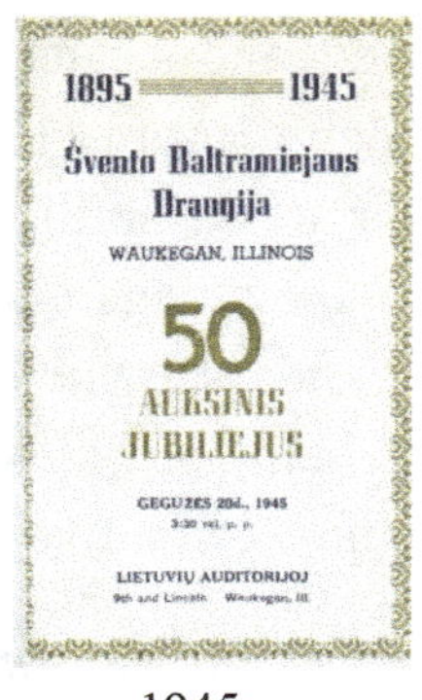
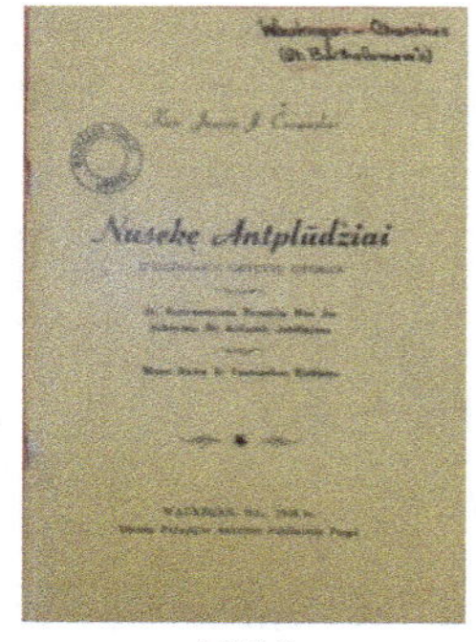

1945   1946
St. Bartholomew Society   St. Bartholomew Parish History
50th Jubilee

Past presidents of the St. Bartholomew Society included:

Kazimieras Vaitekūnas	1894-1907
Antanas Rimkus	1907-1908
Ignacas Kuica	1908-1909
Cyprijonas Janužis	1909-1910
J. Jesulūnas	1910-1914
Alekas Jankauskas	1914-1917
Antanas Bakshis	1917-1920
Alekas Jankauskas	1921-1925
Feliksas Sedarevičius	1926-1928
Benediktas Mačiulis	1928-1930
Jonas Jakutis	1930-1931
L. Zigas	1931-1932
Antanas Sutkus	1932-1935
S. Tauchas	1935-1936
Antanas Sutkus	1936-1943
Charles Vasilius	1943-1945
Antanas Sutkus	1945

The parish continued to host several social and service groups and societies that supported the church and the community. In 1946:

> St. Bartholomew's, with about 160 members; St Joseph's also about 160 members; St. Anthony's – has 130 members; the Holy Name Society has 160 members; The Immaculate Conception of the Virgin Mary with 50 members. St. Ann's with 170 members, The KLRSA has 171 members; the Altar and Rosary Society; Living Rosary and the Perpetual Rosary, Pray Groups; and St. Therese Altar Decoration Group.[24]

Jackson School was the public school alternative located just north or St. Bartholomew Church. The school opened in 1921 and served the community until 1976. The school offered kindergarten through 8th grade. Jackson School was viewed by some as offering a better education than that available at St. Bartholomew. This claim is debatable because there are no objective measures available for comparison. What would not be debatable would be the comparison of a free public education versus the tuition-based education at St. Bart's. The cost of a religious education was offset by the discipline provided by the nuns.

---

[24] Juozis Čužaukas, Nusekę Antplūdžiai Waukegan'o Lietuvių Istorija, page 6.

Jackson School
707 South Jackson St.
Waukegan, IL

In late 1948 and early 1949 Lithuanians displaced by WWII began to be allowed entry into the United States. These immigrants infused the Waukegan community with new members who made significant contributions to the growth and vitality of the community. These immigrants are discussed in more detail in the next section.

This class was confirmed in recent rites at St. Bartholomew church. Front row, left to right, Elizabeth Vasilius, Joyce Hanila, the Rev. F. Lakosius, the Rev. Joseph Cuzauskas, pastor, Susan Jakaitis, Elizabeth Rubar; second row, Anthony Burba, Peter Banis, Edward Rumpelis, Donald Van Heirseele, Therese Wal- rah, Audrey Daujotas, Joseph Lauraitis, Bruno Snaukstas, Gerald Swada, Robert Clark; third row, Robert Jenkins, Daniel Gust, Norbert Petroskis, Mark Vander Vere, Theodore Stanulis, and, in back holding the processional cross, Martin Beus.

St. Bartholomew 1951 Confirmation Class

The Lithuanian community looked for ways to celebrate their heritage and share their culture with the greater community.

Quite colorful will be the costumes of the Lithuanian dancers who will appear in the pageant of North Chicago Days Sunday evening. Under the direction of Roman Saulius the dance will be given by (pictured, left to right): Elizabeth Timcikas, George Barby, Sigute Jan- usonyte, Joseph Salkauskas, Regina Lusaite, Frank Kavalunas, Aldona Listanderyte, Roman Saulius, Stella Tamasauskas, and Jerry Kavalunas. Louis Montrimas is the accordion player.

Waukegan News-Sun photo

Circa 1952

Virginija Kruzikaite and Onute Miliauskaite
February 16, 1965

When St. Bartholomew's School was built in 1909 it included classrooms for the students and living quarters for the nuns. In 1968 the parish built a new convent for the sisters so that they could have a home separate from their students.

Sr. Ann Baubin, Sr. Helen Therese, Sr. M. Clarita, Sr. M. Edwarda, and
Fr. Stanley Jonelis
1968 Ground Breaking Ceremony for New Convent

The societies of the parish supported the school in a variety of ways. A typical example was a fund-raiser bake sale held in the school basement.

St. Bartholomew School Bake Sale
Waukegan News-Sun
October 23, 1970

In 1976 the members of St. Bartholomew parish celebrated the 80th anniversary of the establishment of the parish. Part of the festivities included a mass that was concelebrated by Bishop Alfred Abromowicz of the Chicago Archdiocese, priests ordained from St. Bartholomew and former associates. The festivities were capped by a dinner-dance attended by over 600 current and former members of the parish.[25]

---

[25] St. Bart's Marks 80 Years, Waukegan News-Sun, September 18,1976

St. Bartholomew 80th Anniversary Mass
1976

St. Bartholomew Church
Christmas 1980

Fr. Zavaski

Following WWII when the service men came home, they married and often moved out of the "old neighborhood." A transition began that profoundly changed the nature of the community. Instead of being focused around St. Bartholomew Church, the linkage was to remaining family. The children of many GIs began attending schools and churches in their new locales. These activities are discussed later in the Lithuanian American Community of Lake County section of this paper.

Enrollment at St. Bartholomew school, and all the Catholic schools in the area, declined to the point where new strategies needed to be developed. Father Bill Zavaski, the last pastor at St. Bart's wrote:

> The archdiocese had encouraged parishes to work together to keep Catholic schools surviving in the early 90's. The parishes in Waukegan and North Chicago took that challenge seriously. The pastors of Mother of God (Slovenian) in North Chicago, St. Joseph (German/Hispanic), St. Bart's (Lithuanian) and Holy Family in North Chicago came together to think about how we could keep the schools open for all our people. It was then that the current Lake Shore Catholic Academy came into existence. In 1984 we closed St. Bart's joined Lake Shore Catholic Academy. Lake Shore Catholic . . . . was a model for the diocese at the current time about how to save Catholic schools when the population starts to dwindle . . . . I do remember that what we turned the school into was a social hall for parish meetings, a soup kitchen for the local needy, and a retreat center for the kids attending Lake Shore Catholic Academy . . . . When we closed the school we had a special mass and ceremony and invited all the alumni of the school to join us and after mass all the folks went out of church and hugged the building good-bye. It

was a most memorable moment for all the participants![26]

August 28, 1984
Waukegan News-Sun

SAINT BARTHOLOMEW PARISH   **EIGHTH STREET AND LINCOLN AVENUE**

Established in 1896 to serve the religious needs of Lithuanian immigrants, the history of the Saint Bartholomew Parish is a history of its people, the religious and lay leaders, whose works and accomplishments helped shape the development of the south side of Waukegan. The area surrounding the parish was a development known as Washburn Springs and it was at this location that the immigrants established their homes. Replacing a wooden structure which burned, the new Church, a modern Gothic structure built in 1937, cost $73,000 including furnishings. The Church during the past two years has undergone extensive remodeling, combining the old with the new. The vivid colors of the stained glass windows found throughout the Church are artistically executed and are a dramatic contrast to the pastel mosiacs, statuary and paintings. Mark Konchan, Music Minister, will play the pipe organ intermittently during the tour, and you will be greeted by guides wearing authentic Lithuanian costumes. **Note:** To accommodate its parishioners, the Church will be on view beginning at 1:00 p.m. through 5:00.

St. Bartholomew Parish
1985 Tour of Homes

---

[26] Fr. Bill Zavaski letter to Robert Bakshis September 9, 2017

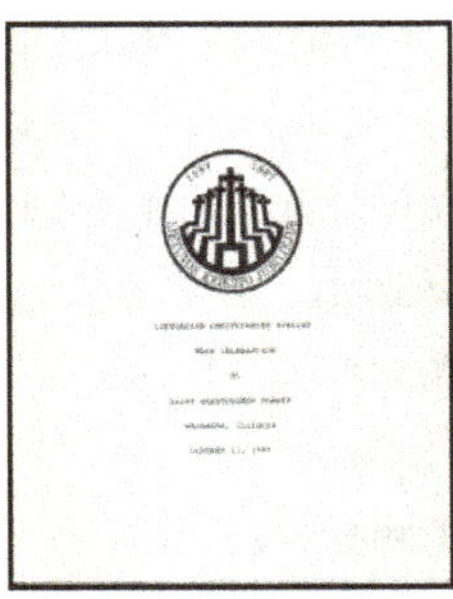

SAINT BARTHOLOMEW RECTORY   730 SOUTH LINCOLN

A very practical addition to the Saint Bartholomew Church was its beautiful red brick rectory constructed in 1930 and dedicated in 1931. The rectory is the home and private quarters of the Church pastor and, through the decades, was filled with visiting dignitaries, neighboring priests and seminary students. The Reverend William Zavaski, pastor, has graciously consented to open his "home" to the public along with the Church. He will have on display a collection of Crucifixes as well as other art work from around the world. Lithuanian artifacts from the Church and private collections dating to the 1800's will be displayed throughout the rectory. The aroma and taste of baked goods indigenous to the Lithuanian culture will await you. A modest structure, you will admire the functional use for which the building was designed. The rectory with its 14 rooms is still occasionally a "home away from home" for seminarians. **Note:** To accommodate its parishioners, the rectory will be on view beginning at 1:00 p.m. through 5:00.

St. Bartholomew Parish
1985 Tour of Homes

Historically, Lithuania was the last European country to accept Christianity. On October 11, 1987 St. Bartholomew Church hosted its last major celebration of Lithuanian culture. A mass was held to celebrate the 600th anniversary of Lithuania's conversion to Christianity.

Mass Program

Baptism of Lithuania
Wojciech Gerson (1831–1901)

Between 1870 and 1904 the Archdiocese of Chicago established five national churches to serve Waukegan's diverse immigrant communities.

1870 - St. Joseph's at McKinley St. and Oak St. to serve the German community.

1896 - St. Bartholomew at 8th St. and Lincoln St. to serve The Lithuanians.

1902 - Holy Family at Argonne Dr. and Lincoln St. in North Chicago to serve the military personnel at Great Lakes.

1903 - Mother of God at 10th St. and McAlister St. to serve immigrants from Croatia, Slovenia and Slovakia.

1904 - Holy Rosary at 14th St. and Victory St. in North Chicago to serve the Polish community.

During the 1980's the Archdiocese of Chicago recognized that demographic changes required that these parishes needed to be reorganized. In 1991 St. Bartholomew Parish and St. Joseph Parish were united as "Saint Joseph and Saint Bartholomew Parish East" and "Saint Joseph and Saint Bartholomew Parish West". Holy Family Parish in North Chicago was closed as was Mother of God in Waukegan. Parishioners from these parishes were encouraged to join parishioners of Holy Rosary under the name "Queen of Peace Parish."

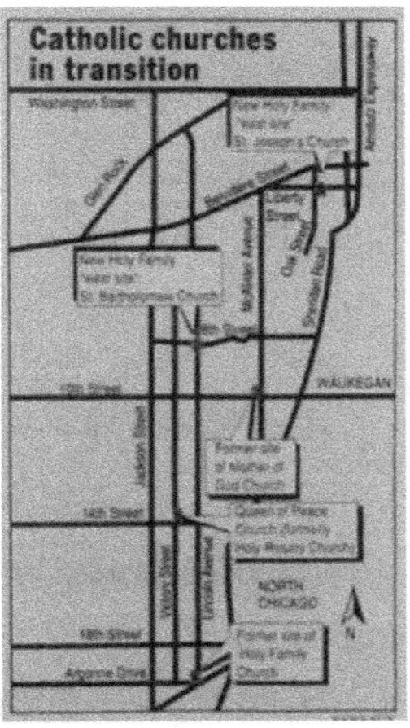

Waukegan News Sun April 20, 1986

The changes did not happen without turmoil. St. Bartholomew parishioner Gediminas Damasius wrote in a letter to the church outlining the concerns of the community.

> I heard from Aldona and Elena about some of the changes which are being considered for the St. Bartholomew-St. Joseph Parish. While change is inevitable, two of the proposed changes are worrisome to me, a member of St. Bartholomew for just thirty four years; they must be devastating to the older parishioners whose parents built the church nearly one hundred years ago. I refer to the proposals which would delete "St. Bartholomew" from the parish name and would abolish the Sunday Mass in Lithuanian.

I would strongly oppose these changes. To me they seem illogical and insensitive. As I understand it, the push for the name change comes from the new parishioners. I understand that they are a large majority in number. I welcome the newcomers as we were welcomed into the parish. I do not see any need or logic for changing the parish name. Does this mean that if any group who joins any parish and becomes a majority can vote to change the name of that parish? I do not think that the Church is that democratic.

I would also plead that you allow me and some of the other parishioners to worship in Lithuanian as we have done all of our lives by keeping one Sunday Mass in our language.

I know I speak for a very small minority within the parish. I know that the needs of their majority are overwhelming. I want to make certain that if the changes are made, that you and the Diocese not be misinformed about the feelings of the original parishioners.[27]

In 1996 the inevitable happened. "Saint Joseph and Saint Bartholomew Parish East/West" was renamed "Holy Family

---

[27] Letter from Gediminas Damasius to Father Gary. December 20, 1995

Parish." Church services were moved a newly acquired Holy Family Church at 540 Keller Ave. in Waukegan. St. Joseph Church was shuttered and St. Bartholomew Church was rededicated as a community center. Stained-glass windows from St. Bartholomew Church were removed and installed at the new Holy Family facility. Plaques acknowledging Lithuanian patrons were mounted near the windows.

St. Bartholomew Christian Life Center[28]   Lithuanian Stained-Glass Windows at Holy Family Church[29]

The closing of St. Bartholomew Church created a void in the lives of the parish's Lithuanians. The bond between being an ethnic Lithuanian and a religious Catholic had been strong for centuries. The Waukegan-Lake County community struggled with the removal of a major aspect of their lives: Catholic mass in the Lithuanian language. The group worked tirelessly to renew that bond. The first religious classes at Gediminas Lithuanian Culture School brought a new enthusiasm and drive to reestablish a Lithuanian mass in Northern Illinois. In 2004 Gediminas Damasius and Gediminas School principal Irena Rutkauskiene reached out to Fr. Jaunius Kelpsa to stress the importance of again

---

[28] "© Augustinas Zemaitis - http://global.truelithuania.com"
[29] "© Augustinas Zemaitis - http://global.truelithuania.com"

having a mass held entirely in Lithuanian in this area. In the same year, after a long break, mass was once again offered in the Lithuanian langage at Saint Joseph Church in Libertyville.

Nerijus Šmerauskas and Violeta Rutkauskiene (school parent commitee president) worked hard to bring back mass services and have first communion classes offered to the children at Gediminas Culture School. The following years mass and first communion was held at Saint Patrick Church in Wadsworth Illinois as well as Santa Maria Del Popolo Chapel in Mundelein Illinois. Lithuanian mass service was held by Fr. Jaunius Kelpšas and Fr. Gediminas Jankūnas.

In 2009 after hefty moral support from the Lake County Waukegan Community members of the community greeted Archbishop Sigitas Tamkevičius, archbishop of Kaunas. He visited with community members at Saint Mary Seminary in Mundelein Illinois, where mass was held to commemorate the centennial of Lithuania.

Eight years after St. Bartholomew parishioner Gediminas Damasius wrote in a letter to the church expressing the concerns of the Lithuanian community; and following many efforts from Lithuanian community, their goal was achieved. In the fall of 2013 Chicago Cardinal Francis George made a decision to establish Our Lady of Siluva Lithuanian Catholic Mission at Santa Maria del Populo in Mundelein. The development of the Mission received enourmous support from Lithuanian Bishop, Rimantas Norvila, other Lithuanian religious leaders as well as the Brighton Park church followers.

Since December 16, 2013 Lithuanian mass is held by Fr. Gediminas Keršys regularly every second Sunday of the month at 2 P.M.

Santa Maria del Popolo Church
116 North Lake St. - Mundelein, IL

DECREE
Establishing a Lithuanian Catholic Mission

Upon consultation with representatives of the Lithuanian Catholic community and in view of the value of public associations of the Christian Faithful and with concern for the spiritual needs of every segment of our Catholic population,

I, Francis Cardinal George, Archbishop of Chicago, hereby establish the Our Lady of Siluva Lithuanian Mission as a public association of the Christian Faithful in the Archdiocese of Chicago for the purpose of operating and maintaining a Mission that is to provide for the religious and pastoral care of Roman Catholics of the Lithuanian ethnic community in our midst, particularly those residing in the more northerly areas of the Archdiocese.

This Mission shall be located in Mundelein Illinois at 116 North Lake Street on the grounds of Santa Maria del Popolo Parish, using the chapel presently being utilized there for various parish functions.

The operation of this Mission shall be the responsibility of a priest director who shall be the Pastor of Nativity of the Blessed Virgin Mary Church in Chicago.

With this Decree, I also approve the proposed statutes for Our Lady of Siluva Lithuanian Catholic Mission which are herein attached.

With my prayers that Our Lord may bless this endeavor and the Blessed Virgin Mary may favor this house in her honor.

Given in Chicago Illinois on the 30th day of Sept. , 2013 , the Feast of St. Lawrence Martyr :

Francis Cardinal George, O.M.I.
Archbishop of Chicago

Msgr. Richard Sanchi
Ecclesiastical Notary

Displaced Persons

Following WWII many Lithuanians came to the United States as displaced persons. The first group of displaced persons included 138 Lithuanians. They arrived in New York on October 30, 1948, on the ship USS General Black.

USS General Black

In the following two years, 27,087 Lithuanian refugees entered the country and about 100 families settled in Waukegan. Many of these families quickly relocated to Chicago where there was a larger Lithuanian presence. Most of the arrivals were met by representatives of the United American Lithuanian Relief Fund. Many of the newcomers were given shelter and jobs by the earlier Lithuanian immigrants.[30]

---

[30] Robertas Salenis, Lithuanians in America: A Historical Sketch, Lituanus – Lithuanian Quarterly Journal of Arts and Sciences, Volume 17, No.4 – Winter 1971

After the Second World War - displaced persons arrived in the community and began to organize. On October 10, 1949 they convened a general meeting. On May 5, 1950 they bought an "Underwood" typewriter for $53 and on June 11, 1950 minutes of their meeting noted that it was decided to organize and named themselves the "Waukegan Apylinkės Lietuvių Tremtinių Būreliu." (Waukegan District Lithuanian Deportees Society.) The deportee's Board proposed to set up an operation plan for the Board and all the exiles should work closely with local Lithuanians and their organizations.

Also, the Board proposed to raise the issue of the introduction of the membership fee. On September 24, 1951 at a general meeting the Center's Board of Directors unanimously decided to affiliate with the Lithuanian Deportees Illinois Community organization. From 1951 to 1956 the names of Lithuanian exiles were recorded. Including full-fledged members and family there were considered to be 93 persons in Waukegan.[31]

This group differed from earlier immigrants in that they were political refugees. In pre-war Lithuania they were doctors,

---

[31] Edward Skalisius, Lithuanian American Community of Waukegan-Lake County, Illinois, 2006

lawyers, teachers, and other professional positions of influence. During the war these people were removed from Lithuania by the Germans. Many men were impressed into service to the Third Reich. Their families were placed in detention camps in Latvia, Poland, Germany, Austria, and Czechoslovakia to assure loyalty to the German Reich. Following the WWII, the communist Lithuanian government did not want these people to return to their homes and blocked their readmission to Lithuania.

Charlie Schapals journey to Waukegan illustrates the story of displaced persons.

> Now halfway through the year to his 81st birthday, Schapals has survived two world wars, a detention camp, the adjustment to a new life in the United States and a number of jobs. Retiring from the News-Sun this week. His life has centered around work, family and a determined dislike for Communist Russia.
>
> Born in 1909 in Glal, a village of approximately 100 in the southwestern part of Lithuania, Schapals grew up with three sisters and a brother on a 40-acre farm where labor was a way of life. His education ended at the grade school level and he worked year around, not only on the family plot but other farms in the area.

No actual combat occurred in Lithuania during World War I, but as an 8-year old he remembers German soldiers staying at his grandfather's house. World War II was different. Although not drafted because he had lost half of his left forefinger and the tip of the middle finger in a thrashing machine accident, Schapals was hauled off by the Germans to a farm in that country.

When the war ended, he was placed in an American detention camp. Life there was more work than stern confinement. His "escape" came when an aunt in Racine, Wis. agreed through proper government channels to bring Schapals in this county.

…. Schapals would like to return to Lithuania to see his brother, sister and 36 year old son, who still works on the family farm. "If they were free, I'd go." He said. "But if it's communist, I don't go. I had friends who worked with me in Germany, and they went back in Lithuania and the Russians put them in Siberia."[32]

---

[32] Waukegan News-Sun, December 28, 1989

Charlie Schapals

There were Lithuanians who had been exiled to Siberia by the Russians in the 1940's who were allowed to return to Lithuania, but found that their homes had been either destroyed during the war or had been taken over by others. One such woman was Anelė Shimulinas-Bakshis. She and her husband Antanas had come to America in the early 1900's. Antanas served as president of the St. Bartholomew Society from 1917-1920. They "made their fortune" working in Waukegan's steel mill and returned to Lithuania before WWII. They used money earned in America to buy land in Lithuania. At that time land purchases were limited to a maximum of 60 hectares per person. Antanas bought 60 hectares of land for himself and 60 hectares of land for Anelė's father. Being a large land owner, Anthony was elected president of the local Farmer's Union. When the Russians purged Lithuania of its 'elites' Anthony and Anelė were among an estimated 350,000 Lithuanians shipped off to exile in Siberia where Antanas died in 1942. Russian policies toward exiles changed in 1954 and the exiles were released from Siberia and some were allowed to return to their homes. Returning to Lithuania, Anelė was not able to reclaim her land. Destitute, she came back to Waukegan to live with relatives until her death in 1978.

Antanas Bakshis

In addition to welcoming displaced persons and giving political support to the captive nation of Lithuania, the Waukegan-Lake County community supported their families that were left behind in the old country. Packages of goods, food, and clothing were shipped to loved ones on a regular basis.

Often letters were mailed at the same time that packages where shipped to alert the recipients regarding what to expect. The packages and letters had to be cleared by soviet censors before delivery. To make it more difficult for censors to steam open letters, egg whites were often applied over the envelope flaps. Once the egg whites had dried, steaming open the flap was almost impossible without damaging the envelope. Even so, the content of the letters and packages were often missing items including money.

Under soviet rule, travelers returning to Lithuania as visitors faced many hurdles. Travel to Lithuania was routed through Moscow. Layovers were often several days in length and required lodging in state-sponsored hotels. Privacy in the hotel rooms was not expected. One traveler reported that they tested soviet surveillance by complaining about a headache while in their room. In the morning the desk clerk inquired if their headache was better.

Once cleared for travel to Lithuania the visitors were limited to stays in either Vilnius or Kaunas. Travel outside the cities was restricted. Families and friends were required to travel to Vilnius or Kaunas to visit. Persons caught traveling outside the city were subject to arrest and deportation and their relatives could also be punished.

Waukegan-Lake County Lithuanian American Community

In order to address their unique situation better, Waukegan's displaced Lithuanians formed their own social and political action committee within the local community. The "Waukegan Apylinkės Lietuvių Tremtinių Būreliu." (Waukegan District Lithuanian Deportees Society) was formed. As the group developed, it affiliated with other groups nationally and became known as the Lithuanian American Community, Inc.

The national LAC was incorporated on February 15, 1952.

> On January 20, 1953 the Waukegan Apylinkės Lietuvių Tremtinių Būreliu joined the Lithuanian American Community (LAC). The national LAC had been incorporated on February 15, 1952. On February 25, 1954 the Waukegan district decided to become an official US Lithuanian LAC affiliate.[33]

For many years the LAC worked in concert with the existing social groups of St. Bartholomew parish. But as older members of the community died or dispersed the importance of St. Bartholomew parish and its societies diminished, the LAC became the dominant group to preserve the identity of the Lithuanian community.

---

[33] Edward Skalisius, Lithuanian American Community of Waukegan-Lake County, Illinois

1959 Waukegan Days - Lithuanian Float

For the 1984 celebration of Lithuanian independence in February, Edward Skalisius, spokesman for the Lake County Lithuanian American Community, estimated that 4,000 people in Lake County were of Lithuanian descent. The annual celebration was usually attended by 300 people.[34]

Over time the Lithuanian community dispersed throughout Waukegan and then into Lake, McHenry, and northern Cook Counties. This demographic shift resulted in the 1984 closure of St. Bartholomew's School and then the merging of St. Bartholomew's church with St. Joseph's Church "Holy Family Parish". Identification as a Lithuanian remained strong among the community but the Lithuanian American Community of Lake County (LAC), rather than St. Bartholomew's parish, became the defining organization. Membership to the LAC is open to everyone of Lithuanian descent. As the first and second waves of

---

[34] Lithuanians Set Anniversary Fetes, Waukegan News-Sun, February 11-12, 1984 Page 2C.

immigrants aged and died off the LAC became predominantly persons from the third wave of Lithuanian immigration – immigrants who left the newly independent Lithuania after 1990.

For thirty years the Lithuanian American Community supported Lithuanian independence through political action. Edward Skalisius (a WWII displaced person) worked to have the flag of Lithuania flown over the Waukegan City Hall annually in February as a symbol of the independence that was lost in 1939. Skalisius looked forward to the day when Lithuania would again be independent. In 1992 his dream came true and there was no longer a need to fly the Lithuanian flag in Waukegan.

Edward Skališius

Flag Raising Over Waukegan City Hall – 1968

Lack of flag good sign for Lithuanians

For the first time in more than 30 years, the Lithuanian flag won't fly over Waukegan City Hall on Lithuanian Independence Day this month.

The flag was displayed annually all those years around Feb. 16 in Waukegan to draw attention to the fact that Lithuania — annexed by the Soviet Union in 1940 — wasn't independent.

But since the Baltic nation regained its political freedom, it is no longer necessary, said Edward Skalisius of Waukegan, a leader of the Lake County Lithuanian American community.

"It's time to end the practice," he said. "We used to do it because it wasn't possible to do it in Lithuania. We're grateful to Waukegan because they've done this so many years."

Area Lithuanians will mark their independence day with a commemorative program at 1:30 p.m. Sunday at St. Bartholomew's Church, 730 Lincoln Ave., followed by a cultural program at 2:30 p.m. in the church's Christian Life Center. The event is open to the public.

Regina Narusis of Cary, Ill., vice president of the Lithuanian-American Community, U.S.A., is among the expected speakers.

Lithuania regained its independence on March 11, 1990, but the country's independence day, Feb. 16, dates from 1918. Lake County is celebrating a week early because many members of the community want to take part in Lithuanian independence events next Sunday in Lemont, Ill., and in Chicago, said Skalisius.

The "main event" will be held the afternoon of Feb. 16 in the Lithuanian World Center in Lemont, he said.

Lake County Lithuanians are expected to approve resolutions this week urging the withdrawal of Commonwealth of Independent States troops from Lithuania and American assistance to the country.

News-Sun 2/8-9/1992

Lake County's Lithuanians Mark Quest for Independence

1988   1992

The Lithuanian community continues to celebrate the country's independence in February.

Lithuanian Independence Day Celebration – 1996

Waukegan-Lake County Chapter Board - Elected April 15, 1977
Back: Algimantas Tamasauskas (V.P.), Aldona Kavaliunas (Treasurer), Pranas
Petroliunas (Secretary). Front: Eleonora Kruzikas (V.P.), Sigita Damasius
(V.P.), and Elena Skalisius (President)

In 1984, following the reorganization of the Waukegan and North
Chicago parishes, St. Bartholomew's was selected to serve as the
Christian Life Center. That is a community center designed to
meet the needy. Many residents in the Waukegan-North Chicago
area needed extra help. One new ministry for the center was a
meal and soup kitchen which opened on December 13, 1984 with
eleven volunteers. On the first night 23 people came for a meal.

Over time the number of guests expanded. By April 1989 the need was so great that meals were being offered two nights a week. The meal and soup kitchen at St. Bartholomew's was the only organization in Waukegan that offered meals two nights a week. By 1992 the kitchen served about 120 guests per night. For the year 1992 the kitchen served 10,551 meals to 6,907 adults and 3,644 children.

Other parishes from Lake County joined in at the food kitchen caring for the needy. Among the groups helping out where the 1st Presbyterian Church of Libertyville, Holy Cross Church of Deerfield, Immaculate Conception Church of Waukegan, Our Lady of Humility of Zion, St. Patrick's Church of Wadsworth, 1st Presbyterian Church of Libertyville Youth Group, St. Mark's Lutheran Church of Lindenhurst, St. Paul the Apostle Youth Group of Gurnee, and St. Mary of the Lake Seminary from Mundelein.[35]

---

[35] Feeding the Hungry, Waukegan News-Sun, March 17, 1993 page B1

Winky Hankins, Antionette Backis and Pat Prusila
Feeding the Hungry – 1993

Groups dedicated to the promotion of Lithuanian culture continued in venues in Lake, McHenry, and northern Cook counties outside of Waukegan.

Woodstock Lithuanians – 2002

Dance Group – 'Klumpe' – 2005

Elena Skališius – 1981

With the Lithuanian community moving out of Waukegan to other areas, the Waukegan-Lake County Lithuanian Community began to produce a newsletter 'Žiniaraštis' that was published four times per year. The newsletter eventually grew to eight pages in length with paid advertisements. The print version of the newsletter gave way to technology with e-mail and other web-based announcements. However, to serve members of the community that were not technologically connected, announcements continued to be distributed to selected individuals by mail. By

2018 approximately 250 members received e-mail announcements and an additional 80 members received mailed announcements.

'Žiniaraštis' Editorial Board - December 12, 2004
Paulina Birgiolaitė, Audronė Birgiolienė, Dainius Skripkauskas, Dalė Skripkauskienė, Albimantas Birgiolas, Elena Skališienė and Eduardas Skališius

Community activities expanded to include an annual picnic, sport festivals, and various cultural and dance fairs.

Annual Picnic
August 27, 2017

Family Fitness Night
October 20, 2018

Annual Picnic - July 28, 2018

Annual Picnic - July 28, 2018

Members of the Waukegan-Lake County Lithuanian community chapter have and continued to support Lithuania. The national Lithuanian American Council was established in 1915, and reorganized in 1940. It continues to function as the most vital national representative of the local Lithuanian American communities. Every three years American–Lithuanian voters elect 60 members to the national board. During the last few decades between 1 and 4 Waukegan-Lake County community members have earned seats on the national board at any given time.

Shortly after Lithuanian independence was restored in 1990 the Waukegan-Lake County community attended a meeting with Vytautus Landsbergis. Landsbergis was a signer of the Lithuanian Decalaration of Independence and the first head of state for the newly independent Lithuania.

Aldona Kavaliūniene - Waukegan LAC,
Vytautas Landsbergis, Grazina Landsbergiene-Ručyte
1990

Just as members of the LRKSA (Lietuvių Romos Katalikų Susivienijimas Amerikoje – Lithuanian Roman Catholic Alliance of America) in 1910's and 1920's; and members of the Lovers of Liberty in the 1930's and 1940's, the Waukegan-Lake County LAC is politically active. One of their many responsibilities include the drafting and completing of annual resolutions. This is done in such a way which reflects the year's political climate as well as any additional social problems. The annual resolution is expected to be read in the local chapters and communities during one of the largest community events and voted on for support. After the resolution is finalized, the final draft is sent to various United States goverment representatives.

Following the restoration of Lithuanian independence, steps were taken to assure that the Russians would not again impose their rule. One step was to petition for membership in the North Atlantic Treaty Organization (NATO). Begining in 1994 Lithuanian military forces assisted in NATO operations in Afganistan. Russia was opposed to this petition and imposed economic sanctions on Lithuania. American LAC chapters contacted their representatives in congress to support Lithuania's admission to NATO. In 1997, in response to the appeals of the Lithuanian American community, Illinois' U.S. Senator Dick Durbin responded with a letter of support.

Senator Durbin has the distinction of being the highest ranking Lithuanian-American in the United States government. His mother, Ona Kutkaitė, was brought to the United States from Lithuania at two years of age. Senator Durbin was born and raised in downstate East St. Louis, IL. He was elected to the U.S. Senate in 1996. In 2004 he was elected as the Democratic Party Senate Whip, responsible for ushering legislation through the Senate.

Ultimately with the backing of the United States government, Lithuania achieved full NATO membership in 2004. As a result

Lithuania comitted to providing troops for NATO missions, and NATO placed military units in Lithuania to guard against Russian aggression.

Badge of NATO Forces in Lithuania

RICHARD J. DURBIN
ILLINOIS

COMMITTEE ON THE JUDICIARY

COMMITTEE ON
GOVERNMENTAL AFFAIRS

COMMITTEE ON THE BUDGET

United States Senate

WASHINGTON, DC 20510-1304

364 RUSSELL SENATE OFFICE BLDG
WASHINGTON, DC 20510-1304
(202) 224-2152
TTY (202) 224-8180

230 SOUTH DEARBORN, 38TH FL.
CHICAGO, IL 60604
(312) 353-4952

525 SOUTH EIGHTH STREET
SPRINGFIELD, IL 62703
(217) 492-4062

SUITE 414
MERCANTILE BANK OF SOUTHERN ILLINOIS
123 SOUTH TENTH STREET
MT. VERNON, IL 62864
(618) 244-7441

September 10, 1997

Algirdas & Violeta Rutkowskas
1820 Delany Road, #111
Gurnee, IL 60031

Dear Friends:

Thank you for contacting me to express your support for Lithuanian membership in the North Atlantic Treaty Organization (NATO).

I share your views about this important issue. I have recently written to President Clinton asking that he designate Lithuania to be eligible to receive aid under the NATO Enlargement and Facilitation Act of 1996. I have also cosponsored a resolution expressing the Sense of the Senate that the Baltic nations should be included in NATO.

The appeal outlines the measures that Lithuania, Estonia and Latvia have taken to prepare themselves for NATO membership, which include: establishing civilian control of the military, police, and intelligence services; respecting the territorial integrity of neighbors; making commitments to protect the rights of all citizens; respecting the values and interests shared by NATO members; furthering the principles of NATO; contributing to the security of the North Atlantic area; and accepting the responsibilities, obligations, and costs of NATO membership.

It is clear that these countries have made every effort to meet the standards of NATO membership. There is no doubt that current NATO members would benefit greatly from this new partnership.

I have received many letters like yours, and I will continue to support the inclusion of Lithuania in NATO. Thank you again for your interest. I hope you will feel free to contact me in the future on this or any other issue.

Sincerely,

Dick Durbin
United States Senator

RJD/ma

Interest in serving on the Lithuanian American Council Midwest Board has led to the election of a large number of Waukegan representatives. The 2012 election resulted in the election of four members of the Waukegan-Lake County community to the Lithuanian American Council Board. Those elected were: Regina Narušienė, Gediminas Damašius, Paulius Slavėnas and Ramutis Pliūra.

The 2015 election resulted in the election to the Board of three representatives: Gediminas Damašius, Paulius Slavėnas and Audrius Abrutis.

In 2018 the election results included four members from Waukegan-Lake County. They were: Gediminas Damašius, Palmira Janušonienė–Westholm, Violeta Rutkauskienė, and Gintautas Steponavičius,

The Waukegan-Lake County community has had active participation in the Lithuanian American Midwest District Board as well as holding seats on the national Lithuanian American Council. In 2018 Jolita Vilimienė, a Waukegan-Lake County community board member, was elected to the Lithuanian American Council Midwest Board.

The Waukegan chapter has continued to issue resolutions supporting Lithuanian freedom. The 2018 Resolution reads as follows:

> We, the members of the Lithuanian American Community, Inc. of Waukegan – Lake County, IL

Chapter, assembled here on this 17th day of February, 2018,

Joyfully celebrating the "Act of Reinstating Independence of Lithuania" signed 100 years ago on February 16, 1918, casting off 120 years of occupation by the Russian Empire;

Hereby do state that

Whereas, the independent Republic of Lithuania has been a dependable ally of the United States that has participated in NATO initiatives across Asia, Africa, and Europe,

Whereas, the independent Republic of Lithuania consistently contributes to the security, stability and economic prosperity of the European Union,

Whereas, in order to prevent a trigger of Article 5 of the North Atlantic Treaty, thereby resulting in American military engagement,

We strongly urge President Trump and the United States Congress to:

1. Enforce the provisions of the Magnitsky Act and other Russian related sanctions.

2. Counter Russian cybersecurity breaches, disinformation campaigns, election meddling, money laundering, and hybrid warfare.

3. Continue U.S. participation in NATO air policing and joint training missions in Lithuania, Latvia, and Estonia that protect the security and sovereignty of our Baltic allies.

4. Take appropriate economic, political, and diplomatic action to thwart Russian aggression against the sovereign state of Ukraine and to end the illegal annexation of Crimea.

5. Require regular international safety inspections of the Russian-built "Astravets" nuclear power plant in Belarus, only 30 miles from Lithuania's capital, Vilnius.

6. Object to the Nord Stream 2 pipeline linking Russia to Germany, which seeks to increase Europe's dependence on Russian energy.

7. Honor Lithuania's Centennial by hosting a high level Lithuanian delegation at the White House and sending a U.S. delegation to Lithuania in 2018.

8. Declare July 23, 2018 "Baltic Freedom Day" in honor of "The Welles Declaration" of 1940, by which U.S. Secretary of State Sumner Welles proclaimed the U.S policy of non-recognition of the forced, illegal incorporation of Lithuania, Latvia, and Estonia into the USSR.

Adopted: 17 February, 2018

Gintautas Steponavičius
Presiding Officer

Gintautas Steponavičius
Chapter President
LAC National Bd. Member

Violeta Rutkauskienė
Executive President
LAC National Bd. Member

Jolita Vilimienė
Secretary of Chapter Bd.
Member of LAC Midwest
District Board

Vesta Steponavičiūtė
Vice President
Public Relations—Media

Palmira Janušonienė-Westholm
Assistant Treasurer
LAC National Bd. Member

Paulius Slavėnas
Chapter
Treasurer

Gediminas Damašius
Long-time Member of LAC
National Board of Directors

Elena Skališienė
Vice President
Public Relations—Media

Senator Durbin's response to this resolution reflected his ongoing concerns regarding Lithuanian independence and continued American support for Lithuanian freedom.

RICHARD J. DURBIN

ILLINOIS

DEMOCRATIC WHIP

United States Senate
WASHINGTON, DC 20510-1304

July 9, 2018

Mr. Gintautas Steponavicius
Lithuanian American Community Inc
Waukegan-Lake County, IL Chapter
239 Spring Valley Way
Round Lake, IL 60073-9543

Dear Mr. Steponavicius:

Thank you for contacting me with your concerns about Russian aggression. I appreciate hearing from you.

In March 2014, I introduced a resolution (S. Res. 72) condemning Russian aggression in Ukraine and supporting sanctions against Russia until its actions in Ukraine are halted and reversed. This legislation passed the Senate in 2015. I have supported increased funding for Ukraine, a nation in great need of international assistance. I also have met with the Ukrainian, Russian, Polish, and Baltic officials and have urged the North Atlantic Treaty Organization (NATO) to continue its commitment to European security

In September 2014, Russian President Vladimir Putin failed to abide by the first ceasefire agreement reached in Minsk, Belarus. In February 2015, Russia continued the siege on Ukrainian forces in Debaltseve, flagrantly violating a second cease-fire agreement reached in Minsk.

I wrote to then-Secretary of State John Kerry after this Russian violation, urging him to consider imposing additional sanctions and penalties on President Putin's actions while providing military support to Ukraine. I also wrote to then-President Obama prior to the NATO Summit in July 2016 about the success and Ukraine and resistance to Russian aggression being in the best interest of all NATO member countries.

President Putin has continued to escalate the conflict and undermine decades of established international norms. He maintains Russia's illegal seizure of Crimea and continues provocations against NATO allies, including aggressive military and propaganda strategies and continues to occupy Georgian territory and support separatists in Moldova.

On January 6, 2017, the U.S. intelligence community released an assessment and we learned that President Vladimir Putin personally ordered a campaign to influence the outcome of this election in President Trump's favor. Moscow has been targeting us and our western allies for a very long time, but this most recent attack on our democracy represents a dramatic escalation that cannot be ignored or go unanswered.

The Obama Administration issued significant new sanctions on the Russian Federation that sent a signal to the Kremlin that must now be amplified by Congress. There is bipartisan support for strong additional sanctions against Russia, and I will support that effort every step of the way, including with legislation I introduced to tighten such sanctions. This legislation, the Countering Russian Hostilities Act of 2017 (S. 94), includes comprehensive sanctions on Russia for their cyber intrusions, aggression, and destabilizing activities here in the United States and around the world. This bill was referred to the Senate Committee on Foreign Relations.

I also am a cosponsor of the Russia Sanctions Review Act, which would require congressional oversight of any decision to provide sanctions relief to the Government of the Russian Federation. This legislation was referred to the Senate Committee on Banking, Housing, and Urban Affairs.

I remain deeply concerned about Russia's aggression toward our allies and friends, as well as its attack on our democracy, and I will continue working to combat this aggression to the best of my abilities.

Thank you again for contacting me. Please feel free to keep in touch.

Sincerely,

Richard J. Durbin
United States Senator

RJD/jw

Vesta Steponavičiūtė , Senator Dick Durbin, Gintautas Steponavičius
2017

Gediminas Lithuanian Cultural School

The celebration of the feast day St. Bartholomew and the founding of St. Bartholomew Church became an annual celebration for the Lithuanian community of Lake County. The Lithuanian American Community of Lake County now holds an annual picnic open to all who wish to attend.

During the annual 2002 summer picnic, a group of Lithuanian families reached out to the Waukegan-Lake County community board asking for support to implement a new Lithuanian Saturday school in the northern suburbs of Chicago. This request was met with enthusiasm and overwhelming support from the then acting board members. After a few short months of preparations, the school saw its grand opening during the first weekend of October in 2002. The brand new school: "Gedimino Lituanistinė Mokykla" (Gediminas Lithuanian School) was located at the Libertyville Civic Center, 135 W. Church Street Libertyville, Illinois.

The decision to start classes during the first week of October was no coincidence, as it is at this time that all of Lithuania celebrates national teacher's day. The beginning of the first day of school gathered eager to learn young students. With such a promising number the school's newly elected "parent committee" worked tirelessly to promote the new learning establishment in the Lithuanian newspapers such as "Draugas" and "Amerikos Lietuvis". During this period of time the Lithuanian community still had an operational Lithuanian television program which featured the news of the brand new school formation with the help of the parent committee members. Gedimino Lituanistinė Mokykla became the third active Lithuanian culture school in the Chicagoland area. Due to tireless efforts and encouragement, the first school year ended with 16 student attendees, compared to 11 during the beginning of the school year. The second school year saw an increase in student attendance from 16 to 22 students. The school celebrated its first birthday in October 2003 - a tradition that carries on to this day.

Gedimino Lituanistinė Mokykla
2002   2003

Gedimino Lituanistinė Mokykla
2003 First Anniversary Celebration

The second year of Gediminas Lithuanian Cultural School saw the formation of two new opportunities for cultural enrichment, religious class and folk dance. With the approach of the 12th annual folk dancing celebration, the school once again reached out to the Waukegan-Lake County board for support. This time it was for the investment in obtaining traditional folk dancing costumes for all the students to appropriately represent the school in the celebration. Once again, the request for support was granted, the school received brand new cultural costumes.

Gedimino Lituanistinė Mokykla
2003 Traditional Costumes

With continuous practice and appropriate dress, the school's dance group participated in their first folk dance celebration.

Gedimino Lituanistinė Mokykla
2004 12th Annual Folk Dance Festival
Allstate Arena, Rosemont, IL
Laura Būgelytė, Mantas Ivanauskas, Ernesta Jonotaitė, Ignas Karaliūnas, Elena
Luotė, Gabija Malakauskaitė, Andrius Mikonis, Laura Pabrėžaitė, Milda
Pociūtė, Laura Pitkutė, Rimantas Podinevas, Žukas Poplevičius, Vesta
Steponavičiutė, Martynas Valainis, Paulius Valainis, Gintarė Vilimaitė
Group Director - Irena Rutkauskienė

It is through contributions such as folk dancing costumes and many various supports throughout the years that the Waukegan-Lake County committee has worked alongside the Gediminas Lithuanian Cultural School to promote the school's active agenda.

Gediminas Lithuanian Cultural School leaders from its beginning:

2002-2004 – Parent committee chairman Gintautas Steponavičius
2004-2005 – Principal Irena Rutkauskienė
2005-2006 – Principal Ingrida Špokienė
2006-2011 – Principal Violeta Rutkauskienė
2011-2016 – Principal Giedrė Ramašauskaite
2016-   – Principal Jurita Gonta

The Gediminas Lithuanian Cultural School is a permanent replacement to the old St. Bartholomew Church facility which had been the center of Lithuanian activity for over a century. The Gediminas school is now located within Santa Maria Del Popolo Church, 126 N. Lake Street, Mundelein, IL near to the geographic center of Lake County. Festivities are held each year are similar to those held at St. Bartholomew Church. There are celebrations for the opening of the school year, All Saint's Day, a Fall festival, the Schools' Birthday, Christmas, Lithuanian Independence Day, Užgavenes (Shrove Tuesday), Easter, Mother's day and the end of the school year.

Faculty for the school includes 11 full-time and 1 part-time instructors. Students include first-, second-, and third-generation Lithuanian. During a typical school year there are 50-70 students enrolled. Classes are held once a week for about four hours.

Gedimino Lituanistinė Mokykla
Mundelein, IL
2017

May 31, 2012

February 26, 2017

April 30, 2017

December 17, 2017

April 4, 2013

December 5, 2015

January 5, 2016

October 29, 2017

Waukegan-Lake County Lithuanian Community Millennium Celebration

In 2009 from October 23rd through the 25th Chicago Lithuanians celebrated Lithuania's millennium. According to Wikipedia[36]

The first written occurrence of Lithuania's name has been traced to the Quedlinburg Annals and dated to 9 March 1009.[37] [38] The passage reads:

> "Sanctus Bruno qui cognominatur
> Bonifacius archepiscopus et monachus XI.
> suæ conuersionis anno in confinio Rusciæ et
> Lituæ a paganis capite plexus cum suis
> XVIII, VII. Id. Martij petijt coelos."[39]

> "[In 1009] St. Bruno, an archbishop and
> monk, who was called Boniface, was slain
> by Pagans during the 11th year of this
> conversion at the Rus and Lithuanian border,
> and along with 18 of his followers, entered
> heaven on March 9th."

---

[36] Annals of Quedlingburg.
https://en.wikipedia.org/wiki/Annals_of_Quedlinburg
[37] Baranauskas, Tomas (Fall 2009). On the Origin of the Name of Lithuania. *Lituanus*. 55 (3). ISSN 0024-5089
[38] Richard C. Frucht. Eastern Europe. 2004. p.169 ISBN 1-57607-800-0
[39] Albinus, Petrus Fabricius, Georg. Chronicon Quedlenburgense ab initio mundi per aetates. Retrieved on 2013-09-05

From other sources that describe Bruno of
Querfurt, it is clear that this missionary
attempted to Christianize the pagan
king Netimer and his subjects.[40] However,
Netimer's brother, refusing to accept
Christianity, killed Bruno and his followers. The
historian Alfredas Bumblauskas has suggested
that the story records the first baptismal
attempt in the history of Lithuania.[41]

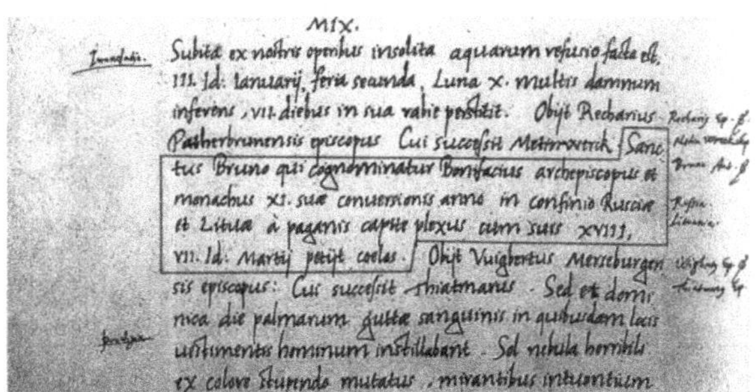

The First Name of Lithuania in Writing – 1009 [42]

This milestone was celebrated by Lithuanians everywhere.
Cultural events and gatherings were held throughout the Chicago
area. For the occasion Chicago was visited by Archbishop Sigitas
Tamkevičius, the archbishop of Kaunas, as well as other
prominent guests. During his time in the city the archbishop was

---

[40] Alfredas Bumblauskas. Lietuvos tūkstantmetis – Millennium Lithuaniae.
     Retrieved on 2009-09-01
[41] Alfredas Bumblauskas. Lietuvos tūkstantmetis – Millennium Lithuaniae.
     Retrieved on 2009-09-01
[42] By Unknown. Most likely a canoness at the Quedlinburg Abbey - Scan from
     Bumblauskas, Senosios Lietuvos istorija 1009-1795, Public Domain,
     https://commons.wikimedia.org/w/index.php?curid=1958066

accompanied by Dr. Irena Vaišvilaitė, advisor to former Lithuanian president Valdas Adamkus, and Nerijus Šmeraukas, former religious course instructor at Gediminas Lithuanian Culture School in Mundelein.

President Valdas Adamkus, Vesta Steponavičiūtė – 2011

On October 24th the school was not only celebrating 1000 years of the Lithuanian name, but also the 7th anniversary of the founding of the school in Mundelein.   At the school, Archbishop Tamkevičius met with the students, their parents, teachers, and many other Lithuanians in the northern suburbs who wished to meet with him.   A good portion of his visit was spent familiarizing himself with the school as well as enjoying a cultural program dedicated to his visit performed by the students of the school.

Millennium Cake

Archbishop Sigitas Tamkevicius

Gediminas Lithuanian Cultural School

Following the school visit the rest of the day's events continued at the nearby St. Mary of the Lake Seminary also located in Mundelein, Illinois. Once again, the archbishop was greeted by a large crowd of Lithuanian followers were a mass was concelebrated with the archbishop, the head of the seminary - Denis J. Lyle, prelate Jurgis Šarauskas, priest Dr. Arvydas Žygas, priest Jaunius Kelpšas and priest Gediminas Jankūnas. This special mass was led by Archbishop Tamkevičius during which, he took the time to concerate the official Lithuanian flag of Gediminas Culture School. The following day the flag was brought by Gediminas school representatives to the Chicago Cathedral where a large scale Lithuanian mass was held. After the mass held at the Mundelein Seminary church goers had a chance to partake in a special lunch where they enjoyed each others as well as the archbishop's company.

Archbishop Sigitas Tamkevicius

Flag of Gediminas
Lithuanian Cultural School

Commemoration of the Darius and Girėnas Flight

On June 18, 1932 Lithuanian American pilots Steponas Darius and Stasys Girėnas purchased a Pacemaker airplane, registered as NC-688E, from the Pal-Waukee Company in Palatine, IL for $3,200.[43] In January the airplane was move to Chicago for extensive refitting and modification. By March 1933 the rebuild was complete, and the registration number was changed to NR-688E. Sponsor's names were painted on the fuselage and the plane was named "Lituanica." The pilots departed Floyd Bennett Airport in New York City headed for Kaunas on July 15, 1933, and crashed over Soldin, Germany on July 17. It was strongly suspected that they were shot down by the Nazi's after they strayed well into German airspace. An investigation however, suggested that storms and rainy weather and fog as the most likely deadly factor in their flight. At the time their 3,984 mile flight ranked as the second longest non-stop flight on record. Their flight was the first to carry trans-Atlantic air mail.

Lituanica over New York City [44]

Crash Site in Germany

---

[43] The Pal-Waukee Company was located at the Palwaukee Airport (now the Chicago Executive Airport) located near Palatine Road and Milwaukee Avenue in Wheeling, IL

[44] By Old newspaper chronics - http://www.lituanica.lt/photos.html, CC BY

Darius and Girėnas were hailed as national heroes and received a large state funeral. Monuments to their achievement have been erected in Kaunas, Vilnius, New York City and Chicago.

Darius and Girėnas
State Funeral - Kaunas

Memorial – Marquette Park
Chicago

When Lithuania regained its independence in 1990 the country needed to print its own currency. Images of Darius and Girėnas were place on the 10 Litų banknote. Over the years the banknote received several modifications until it was ultimately replaced by the Euro. The last version of the banknote featured the words "Mil*waukee and Pal*atine" on Darius' cap.

Lithuania 10 Litų Banknote Detail

In 2013 Lithuanians observed the 80th anniversary of the flight of Darius and Girėnas. At O'Hare International Airport the Ministry of Foreign Affairs of the Republic of Lithuania sponsored a display honoring Darius and Girėnas. This display was presented by the Consul General of the Republic of Lithuania, Vytautas the Great War Museum (Kaunas, Lithuania), Balzekas Museum of Lithuanian Culture (Chicago, IL).

O'Hare International Airport – Chicago, IL
Darius and Girėnas Display
2013

The Waukegan-Lake County community and board members looked for an opportunity to commemorate the flight with a special plaque which celebrated the historical event as well as the place of its possible origin. The W-LC Board determined that the place for such a plaque was the Chicago Executive Airport, previously known as the Palwaukee Airfield.

In the spring of 2013 a committee was formed to take charge in organizing and working with the Palwaukee Airfield administration to allow the hanging of a plaque. This committee consisted of Ronald Westholm (chair), Palmyra Janušonienė-Westholm, Regina Narušienė, Paulius Slavėnas, Auksuolė

Marciulevičienė and Violeta Rutkauskienė. The project was underwritten by the Waukegan-Lake County Lithuanian Community. The committee worked closely with the airport manager Dennis G. Rouleau as well as the executive director Jamie L. Abbott.

On August 19th, 2013 having received the approval from the Chicago Executive Airport, a plaque honoring Darius and Girėnas was dedicated. The dedication of the plaque brought dignitaries of local governments and the Lithuanian community. Guests included the mayor of Prospect Heights Nicolas Helmer, administrative representatives from the city of Wheeling, the Chicago Executive Airport Board, CEA committee members Ray Lang, Nick Katz and Signature Terminal representatives. Republic of Lithuania representatives included: then General Consul of Lithuania in Chicago Marijus Gudynas alongside Consul to-be Mantvydas Bekešius and a small delegation of parliament members of Lithuania led by prime minister Vydas Gedvilas. Those who could not attend, such as Senator Dick Durbin, sent a congratulatory note for the occasion. Other guests in attendance included pilot Linda Uznys, who was very proud to share the same flying license as the two heroic pilots being celebrated. At the time, Linda Uznys had already spent 40 years as a Darius and Girėnas American Legion Post #271 member as well as being a member of the Ninety-Nines: International Organization of Women Pilots. During the ceremony project committee member Regina Narušienė spoke of the profound history of Darius and Girėnas and their achievements in aviation. For the special occasion Violeta Rutkauskienė also released a special commemorative post card.

Now, everyone who passes through the Chicago Executive Airport Signature Terminal can stop to appreciate the plaque that hangs dedicated to the aviation pioneers Darius and Girėnas.

Prospect Heights Mayor Nicolas Helmer, Gen. Counsul of Lithuania Marijus Gudynas, Palmira Janušoniene-Westholm, Paulius Slavėnas, Regina Narušiene, Kristina Kačkuviene, Lithuania Parlament (Seimas) Chairman Vydas Gedvilas, Jonas Prunskis, Auksuolė Marčiuleviciene, Violeta Rutkauskienė

Darius and Girėnas Plaque

Commemorative Postcard

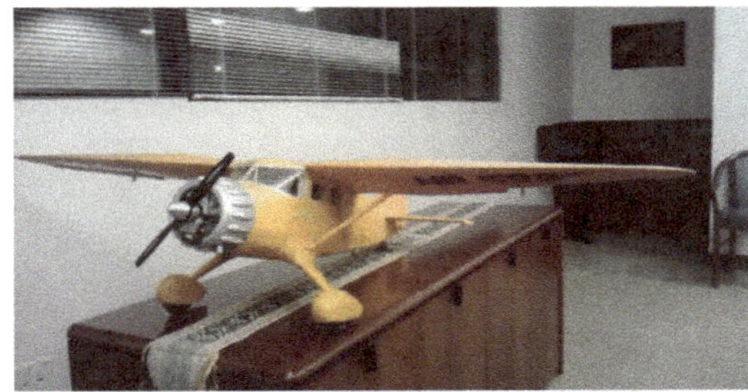

Lituanica Model
Chicago Executive Airport

RICHARD J. DURBIN

ILLINOIS

ASSISTANT MAJORITY LEADER

COMMITTEE ON APPROPRIATIONS

COMMITTEE ON FOREIGN RELATIONS

COMMITTEE ON THE JUDICIARY

COMMITTEE ON RULES
AND ADMINISTRATION

United States Senate
Washington, DC 20510-1304

September 13, 2013

Dear Friends:

Greetings! It gives me great pleasure to welcome all of you to The Lithuanian American Community Waukegan Lake County Chapter's unveiling of the memorial plaque commemorating the 80th anniversary of the transatlantic flight of Darius and Girenas. As you gather to remember the courageous way in which these two men traversed the Atlantic Ocean, you have an opportunity to honor their bravery and sacrifice.

For more than 60 years, the Lithuanian American Community has sought to preserve the Lithuanian cultural identity and pass it on to the next generations. Through the educational, artistic, and cultural programs that you offer, you provide the community an opportunity to engage with Lithuanian culture. I applaud your commitment to making these cultural connections happen.

Again, I would like to extend my warmest wishes to tonight's attendees to your ceremony. Congratulations on all your work and achievements, and I wish you best of luck in your future endeavors.

Very truly yours,

Richard J. Durbin
United States Senator

Lithuanian Independence Centennial Celebration

On March 10, 2018, the Waukegan-Lake County Lithuanian American Community held a gala celebration to recognize the 100th anniversary of Lithuanian independence. Waukegan's Lithuanian community had supported independence since its founding in the 1890's and this support continued through good times and bad. Following WWI Waukegan's Lithuanians celebrated when Lithuanian gained its independence from Germany. Their hopes were dashed when the independent Lithuanian state was absorbed by the Soviet Union. The local chapter of the Lovers of Liberty worked diligently to support family and friends in Lithuania while pursuing their ultimate goal of a free and independent Lithuania. Their work was successful in 1991 when Lithuania regained its independence. In keeping with their activities for over 125 years, the Waukegan-Lake County Lithuanians celebrated their successes and look forward to the future.

The day following the gala celebration (March 11, 2018), the Waukegan-Lake County Lithuanian community commemorated restoration of independence by consecrating a Lithuanian flag at Santa Maria Del Popolo Parish in Mundelein Illinois. March 11, 1918 is the original day of restoration of Lithuanian independence.

The idea was so well received that the Lithuanian consulate located in Chicago was willing to participate in the event. On the day of the consecration the Waukegan-Lake County Lithuanians received a 30-meter long Lithuanian flag first brought to the United States by a signer of the Lithuanian Declaration of Independence and head of the Lithuanian Parliament (Seimas), Vytautas Lansbergis. This much respected flag was lent by the Consulate of the Lithuanian Republic to be blessed at the March 11th ceremony. The 30-meter flag along with many other Lithuanian flags brought by individuals from the community were blessed by Fr. Gediminas Keršys during a mass service.

30-Meter Flag

Vidas Kazlauskas, Ramute Kazlauskas,
Fr. Gediminas Keršys, Valerija Rutkauskienė,
Violeta Rutkauskienė, Algirdas Rutkauskas,
Žaneta Steponavicienė

Centennial Gala Announcement

At the gala, lifetime achievement awards were given to eight worthy members of the Waukegan-Lake County community:

- Birute Baltrus receiving the Honor for an extremely generous donation to the Lake County Lithuanian Community and her unwavering work with the community board. She was unable to attend celebration.

- Gediminas Damasius receiving the Honor for his lifelong commitment to the Waukegan- Lake County Lithuanian Community and outside its borders.

- Palmira Janusoniene–Westholm receiving the Honor for her long serving rigorous work with the Waukegan- Lake County Lithuanian Community.

- Stasys Milasius receiving the Honor for his unwavering commitment to teaching Lithuanian folk dance to the Lithuanians living in the Waukegan – Lake County Lithuanian Community area. He was unable attend the gala celebration,

- Regina Narusiene receiving the Honor for her active participation in the Waukegan- Lake County Lithuanian Community as well as her determined work towards keeping the Lithuanian name relevant in The United States.

- Violeta Rutkauskiene receiving the Honor for her diligent hard work supporting the Waukegan- Lake County Lithuanian Community as well as creating a Lithuanian chapel.

- Elena Skališienė receiving the Honor for over 50 years of heartfelt ongoing work and effort to conserve the Waukegan-Lake County community.

- Remigijus Suziedelis receiving the Honor for his long serving rigorous work with the Waukegan - Lake County Lithuanian Community.

Gediminas Damasius, Remigijus Suziedelis,   Consul Mantvydas Bekesius,
Violeta Rutkauskiene, Consul Mantvydas Bekesius,   Egle Bekesius,
Regina Narusiene, Elena Skališienė,   Sandra Holloway Darius Kairys,
Palmira Janusoniene–Westholm   Gintautas Steponavičius

Other noteworthy members of the community not recognized at the gala were Sigita Damasius and Eduardas Skalisius.

- Sigita Damasius, a long-term member of the LAC, as Board Vice-President seven times, and also served terms are secretary, treasurer, and on the audit committee.

- Eduardas Skalisius was on the Board of the LAC for over 50 years serving 6 terms as President of the Board, 1 term as Vice-President and 22 terms as Political Affairs Head. Mr. Skalisius passed away in 2006.

Dance Group – 'Rusne'

Dance Group – 'Laume'

Members of the dance group Rusne include: Alina Felde, Edita Povilonis, Gabija Slutaite, Danielius Stein, Izabela Stein, Jolanta Stein, Karolina Tuska, Loreta Tuska, Matas Tuska, Indra Verbiejute, Director Nijole Cerniauskiene.

Members of the damce group Laume include: Jurgita Bartkiene, Alina Birenyte, Linas Dailide, Lina Ezerskyte, Ieva Griciute, Dainius Indriliunas, Jashon Jeffries, Ramunas Paulauskas, Lilija Pumputiene, Raimondas Steponavičius, Jolita Vilimiene, Director Vaida Indriliunas.

Darius Kairys

Robert Bakshis, Birute Kairiene -
Lithuanian American Midwest Board President

Lukas Higginbotham

Sakotis – Tree Cake

Vesta Steponavičiūtė, Zaneta Steponavicienė

On September 19, 2018 the City of Waukegan raised the Lithuanian flag in celebration of the centennial of the signing of the Act of Independence. A similar flag-raising had taken place 50 years ago at City Hall. Present at the flag raising were many city officials - including Waukegan Mayor Sam Cunningham, Waukegan City Clerk Janet Kilkelly, Deputy City Clerk David A. Patterson, 2nd Ward Ald. Patrick Seger, Fourth Ward Alderman David Villalobos, Deputy Fire Chief Gene Decker, and Director of Public Relations David Motley. They were given achievement award medals commemorating 1968 event. Helping to mark the occasion were the Consul General of Lithuanian in Chicago Mantvydas Bekesius, Lake County Sheriff Mark Curran, Lake County State's Attorney Mike Nerheim, artist Nele, and members of the Waukegan-Lake County Chapter of the Lithuanian - American Community, Inc.

The LAC group included Elena Skalisius whose husband Edward had organized the original flag raising over Waukegan City Hall in 1968. Elena served as the official photographer in 1968 and took the iconic photo of the event that is featured on the LAC achievement award medal.

Waukegan Mayor - Sam Cunningham,
Consul General of Lithuanian in Chicago - Mantvydas Bekesius,
President of Waukegan-Lake County LAC - Gintautas Steponavičius

Lithuanian Building and Loan Association

Faced with an inability of recent early immigrants to qualify for loans, the Lithuanian community responded by forming their own loan association. On March 24, 1924 the Lithuanian Building and Loan Association of Waukegan was incorporated by the State of Illinois.

By 1953 the Lithuanian Building and Loan Association had outgrown their space in the Lithuanian Hall. A new building was constructed at 10th and Lincoln. They opened in their new location in December 1954 and the name was changed to the Waukegan Savings and Loan Association.

On the 75th anniversary of the association the members were given this history:

> Our founders were Thomas M. Baron, John Bakshis, Alex Jankauskas, Benedict Maciulis, Felix Sedar, Jerome Shimulinas, Matthew Skirius, A.J. Sutkus, William Svitorius and Stanley Zickus. At the end of our first year of operation we had assets of $10,000 and had paid $56.00 in dividends to our savers. During our first two years of existence, we shared offices with Insurance Broker A.J. Sutkus at 1007 Eighth Street. We then moved to a one room office in the Lithuanian Auditorium Building at 901 Lincoln Street, where we remained for twenty-eight years. During this time we had only a part time staff. In December 1954 we

moved to the building we had constructed at 900 Tenth Street – our present home. By this time, we had a full time staff; and the area we served extended to all parts of Waukegan and into the surrounding cities. Our name was changed to the Waukegan Savings and Loan Association . . . . We know that you, as members of Waukegan Savings and Loan, have made it what it is – an Association with assets of over $14 million; planning to pay almost $800,000 in dividends to our savers this year.[45]

The Lithuanian Building and Loan Association became an important engine to the financial vitality of the community. Their initial dividend was 0.56% and grew to 5.71% by 1976. This enabled people to buy homes and establish business while earning a good return on their investment.

In 1995 the Building and Loan Association received a five-star rating by Bauer Financial Reports, Inc. This rating meant that the Association was one of the safest, most credit worth organizations in the country.[46]

In August 2012 the Waukegan Savings and Loan ceased to exist when it was absorbed by the First Midwest Bank.

---

[45] Waukegan Savings and Loan Association letter to member May, 1974.
[46] Waukegan Savings Founded by Lithuanian Americans, Waukegan News-Sun, March 15, 1994.

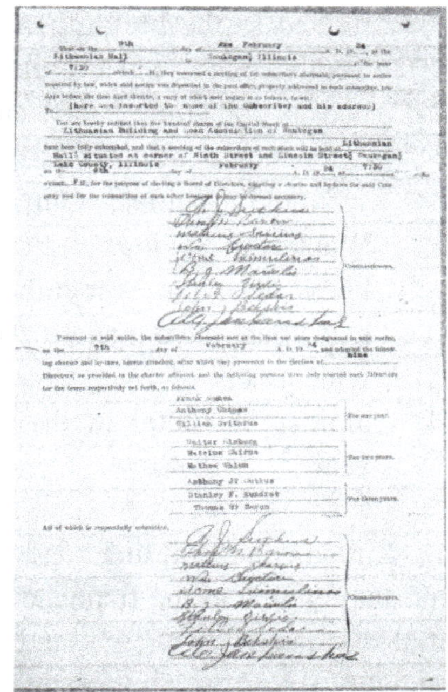

1924 - Lithuanian Building and Loan Association Papers of Incorporation

October 17, 1953

October 19, 1953

Notable Waukegan Lithuanians

Jack Benny

Waukegan's number one "native son" is Jack Benny. He was born Benjamin Kubelsky. His parents were Meyer Kubelsky, a Polish Jew and Emma Sachs Kubelsky, a Lithuanian Jew.[47] Although there is a tie to being Lithuanian, by being Jewish it is unlikely that Benny identified with the predominately Catholic Lithuanian community. In fact the Kubelsky family lived at 910 South Marion Street (now Genesee Street). That would be several blocks north and east of the major Lithuanian group. Benny started his career in Waukegan and later went on to become a mega-star in vaudeville, radio and television. In 1961 the Waukegan Public Schools honored Benny's roots to the city by naming their newest school, Jack Benny Jr. High School, after him. The school has since been renamed Jack Benny Middle School.

Jack Benny

---

[47] Finkelstein, Norman. Jewish Comedy Starts: Classic to Cutting Edge, Kar-Ben Publishing. Minneapolis, MN Copyright 2010

Walter 'Whitey' Budrun

Walter 'Whitey' Budrun (Vytautas Budriūnas) was born December 19, 1908 in Waukegan, IL. At 6'2" and 192 pounds, Budriūnas was a prototype for future players. When he was young he broke his left arm, and it was never set correctly. As a result, he couldn't shoot a basketball using the two-handed method commonly used in the 1930's. He was considered to be a pioneer of the hook shot and the one-handed jump shot. He stared in basketball at Marquette University in Milwaukee, graduating in 1934. Budriūnas was featured in "Ripley's Believe It or Not®" syndicated newspaper series while at Marquette University for scoring nine points in 55 seconds February 1931 versus Fordham University.[48]

In 1939 Budriūnas and several other Lithuanian-American basketball players traveled to Lithuania to play for the Lithuanian national basketball team in the EuroBasketball tournament. The Lithuanian team was undefeated and won the tournament. During the tournament Budriūnas scored 73 of the 396 points (18%) scored by the Lithuanians. In 2007 he was named the fourth most famous Lithuanian basketball player of all time.

---

[48] The News Sun - Waukegan (IL), August 8, 2003

Walter Budrun

Ripley's Believe It or Not ®[49]

EuroBasketball 1939 [50]

Lithuania vs Latvia	37-36
Lithuania vs Estonia	33-14
Lithuania vs Poland	46-18
Lithuania vs France	48-18
Lithuania vs Hungary	79-15
Lithuania vs Finland	112-9
Lithuania vs Italy	41-27

Johnny Dickshot

"Ugly" Johnny Dickshot (John Dicksus) was born January 24, 1910 in Waukegan. He proclaimed himself to be the ugliest man in baseball. At 6' and 195 pounds Dickshot was a formidable presence. Dickshot started his career playing minor league ball with the Milwaukee Brewers in the 1930s. He moved up to the majors and played for the Pittsburgh Pirates (1936-1938) and New York Giants (1939). In 1941 he was

---

[49] "© 2018 Ripley Entertainment Inc."
[50] En.wikipedia.org/wiki/EuroBasket_1939

moved down to the minors where he played for the Hollywood Stars in the Pacific Coast League. In 1943 he hit .352 and had a 33-game hitting streak. In 1945 he was again moved up to the majors with the Chicago White Sox. He hit .302 for the White Sox, had 58 RBIs and 18 stolen bases. His baseball career ended in 1945 with the White Sox. His career batting average was .276 with 7 home runs and 116 RBIs.[51]

Upon retiring from baseball, Dickshot returned to Waukegan and opened Dickshot's Dugout tavern on the corner of 9th and Victory.

 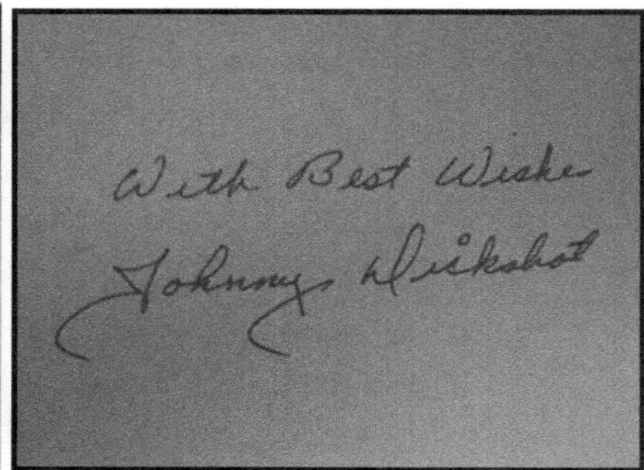

Johnny Dickshot

Alex Kapter

Alex Kapter (Kapterauskas) was born March 26, 1922 in Waukegan. At 6' 205 pounds he was considered to be a large football player at the time. He played football along with future NFL Hall of Famer, and fellow Waukeganite, Otto Graham at Waukegan High School, Northwestern University and the Cleveland Browns.

---

[51] Sports Collectors Digest, December 26, 1997

Kapter played in the College All-Star Game in 1943 and was named to the team again in 1944. The Navy barred him from playing in the 1944 game because of a rule that disallowed any activity that required seamen to be absent 48 hours or more.

In 1944 he was drafted by the Detroit Lions in the 21st round of the NFL draft (211th overall). Because of the war he did not play professional football that year. In 1946 he joined the newly formed Cleveland Browns, where he played right guard. That year the Browns franchise played in the NFL rival All-American Football Conference (AAFC). The Browns finished the season by winning the conference championship defeating the New York Yankees 14-9.[52] The players split the gate receipts. The championship team received 60% of the gate receipts with each player earning $931.57.[53]

In 1950 the Browns joined the NFL.

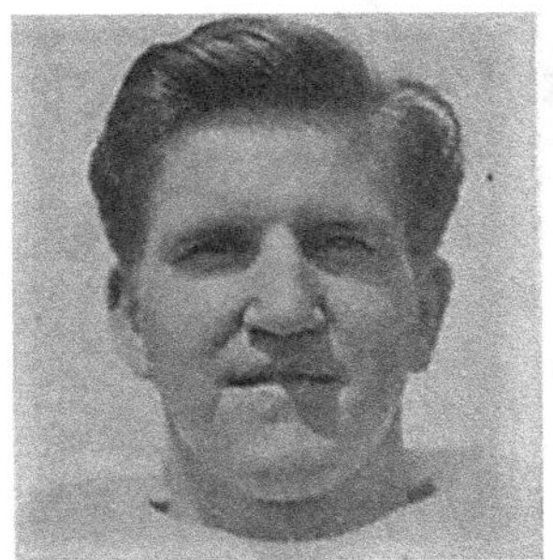

Alex Kapter

---

[52] http://goldenrankings.com/AAFCchampionshipGame1946.htm
[53] $931.57 in 1946 equals $10,885.63 in 2018

Patrick Nugent

On December 25, 1965 Waukegan was excited to learn the news that Patrick Nugent was engaged to be married to Luci Baines Johnson, the daughter of President Lyndon Baines Johnson. Nugent was of Irish-Lithuanian descent. The Nugents lived on Prescott Ave. in the heart of the Lithuanian neighborhood. Patrick was a graduate of St. Bartholomew's school. On August 6, 1966 Fr. John Kuzinskas, St. Bartholomew's pastor, officiated the marriage at the Basilica of the National Shrine of the Immaculate Conception in Washington, D.C.

Johnson-Nugent Wedding

Jerry Orbach

Jerry Orbach was born in the Bronx, NY. His father Leon Orbach was a German Immigrant from Hamburg, Germany who was descended from Sephardic Jews. His mother Emely Olexy was born in Pennsylvania of Polish-Lithuanian parents. Orbach's parents moved frequently, but settled in Waukegan, IL where they lived at 420 McKinley Ave. St. Joseph's Catholic Church (the "German" church) was located just two blocks east of the Orbach home. Jerry graduated from Waukegan Township High School in 1952.

Jerry Orbach was a star of television, stage and screen. He was inducted into the American Theater Hall of Fame (1999). He also received a Screen Actors Guild Award for Outstanding Performance by a Male Actor in a Drama Series (2005) for his longtime role in the TV drama series "Law & Order."

Jerry Orbach

Military Service

During WWI, WWII, Korea, Vietnam and the Gulf Wars, the Lithuanians of Waukegan stepped forward to serve America.

In WWI many of these soldiers thought that by serving in Europe that they would have an opportunity to return to Lithuania to visit. That generally did not happen. One Lithuanian-American, Sgt. Peter Kaminskis served under General George Pershing in France. Kaminskis was shot on Armistice Day, November 11, 1918, and died the following day. Funeral services were held at St. Bartholomew Church. He was buried at Mt. Olivet Cemetery in Waukegan.   His remains were later reburied in Ascension Cemetery, Libertyville, IL

Sgt. Peter Kaminskis

Funeral – St. Bartholomew's

During WWII Waukegan's Lithuanians again stepped forward, serving in all the branches of the military. Peter Motiaytis, originally of Worcester, Mass, was a gunner on a B-17 bomber that was shot down on a mission over Schweinfurt, Germany. Of the 291 Flying Fortresses on the mission 60 were lost and only 33 returned to base without damage. Because of the large loss of planes and crews, this raid occurred on what is now called "Black Thursday". Peter and three other crewmates, including Charles Jellings from Waukegan, managed to bail out of their damaged plane near Wurzburg, Germany and survive. They were captured by the Germans on October 14, 1943 and spent the next 610 days in the infamous Stalag 17-B POW camp near Krems, Austria. Military records report that he was beaten while being held prisoner. Following the war Motiaytis and Jellings returned to Waukegan where Motiaytis married, raised a family and lived for the next 66 years.

Back L-R: Lt. Kenneth Elbert Gross (B); Lt. Jerome Fraser Hart (N),
Lt. Marion Dale Odell (CP),Lt. Lawrence "Larry" Keller, Jr. (P)
Front L-R: Sgt. Vigilio D. Jacoby (TT), Sgt. Peter Charles Motiaytis (FG),
Sgt. Wallie Hayes Vansandt, Jr.(RO), Sgt. Harold Keith McClean (BT),
Sgt. John Edward Maloney (FG), Sgt. Charles Albert Jellings (TG),
Sgt. Norbert Francis Philippi (FG)

Among those who died during the war were six Waukegan-Lake County Lithuanian-Americans: Pvt. Stanley Akramas, Pvt. Frank Bakshis, S/Sgt. Raymond Bujan, Sgt. Charles Gudonis, Pvt. Frank Mazaitis, and Pvt. Simon Pocius.

Pvt. Akramas served with the 4th Infantry Division, 8th Infantry Regiment. On D-Day the 4th Infantry Division was the first to land on Utah Beach. Pvt. Akramas was killed in action several months later on September 22, 1944 during the Battle of the Bulge. Pvt. Akramas was awarded the Silver Star, Purple Heart with Oak Leaf Clusters, Combat Infantryman Badge, American Campaign Medal and the WWII Victory Medal. He was originally buried at Temporary Cemetery Fosse, Belgium. Later his remains were moved to the Henri-Chapelle Cemetery near Liege, Belgium.

Pvt. Bakshis served in the 5th Army under General Mark Clark. He had been wounded in action near Salerno, Italy. He was about to return to duty, but died of wounds when the field hospital he was at was shelled by "friendly fire" killing him on February 21, 1944. He was awarded the Purple Heart. His body was returned to the United States. Funeral services were held at St. Bartholomew Church. He was buried at Mt. Olivet Cemetery in Waukegan.   His remains were later reburied in Ascension Cemetery, Libertyville, IL

S/Sgt. Bujan served in Company C of the 23rd Armored Infantry Battalion, 7th Armored Division.   Initially S/Sgt. Bujan was reported as missing in action on April 10, 1945. Three weeks later, on May 2nd the War Department reported that S/Sgt Bujan had been killed by rocket and artillery fire on April 10th. He was awarded the Purple Heart, Combat Infantry Badge, European Campaign Medal with two Battle Stars, the American Campaign Medal, and the WWII Victory Medal. His body was returned to the United States. Funeral services were held at St. Bartholomew Church. He was buried at Mt. Olivet Cemetery in Waukegan. His remains were later reburied in Ascension Cemetery, Libertyville, IL.

Sgt. Gudonis died from wounds on May 5, 1945 while serving on Luzon in the Philippines under General Douglas MacArthur. He had served 2 ½ years in the Pacific theater. He was previously wounded on February 10th, but had returned to action in April. He was awarded a Purple Heart with Oak Leaf Clusters. His body was returned to the United States. Funeral services were held at St. Bartholomew Church. He was buried at Mt. Olivet Cemetery. His remains were later reburied in Ascension Cemetery, Libertyville, IL.

Pvt. Mazaitis was a member of the 129th Infantry Division which served in the Philippines under General Douglas MacArthur. He was killed in action on April 21, 1945. He is buried at the Manilla American Cemetery, Teguig City Philippines. He was awarded a Purple Heart.

Pvt. Pocius' died July 23, 1943 when a government truck rolled over on him at Camp Forrest, Coffee, TN. According to records, he was killed instantly from traumatic shock. His body was returned to Waukegan. Funeral services were held at St.

Bartholomew Church. He was buried at Mt. Olivet Cemetery. His remains were later reburied in Ascension Cemetery, Libertyville, IL.

Pvt. Stanley Akramas

S/Sgt. Raymond Bujan

Pvt. Frank Bakshis

Sgt. Charles Gudonis

Two plaques were mounted at the entrance to Lithuanian Hall listing the names of all WWII service men from the community. Stars were place next to the names of those who had died.

Fortunately there were no casualties among those who served in Korea, Vietnam, or the Middle East conflicts that followed.

In the mid-1950s the American Can Corporation needed to expand their operation. Their factory was located on Dugdale Avenue adjacent to Mt. Olivet Cemetery. The cemetery was only a couple of blocks north of the Lithuanian neighborhood, and was the 'final resting place" of many Lithuanians, including WWI casualty Kaminskis and WWII casualties Bakshis, Bujan, Gudonis, and Pocius. The cemetery was declared to be in a state of neglect and was deemed "abandoned". In 1958 there were about 1,000 graves at Mt. Olivet. The graves with identified bodies were moved to either St. Mary's Cemetery on Genesee St. in Waukegan or Ascension Cemetery in Libertyville. The remains of 600 unidentified bodies were to be moved to St. Mary's cemetery.

Mt. Olivet Cemetery

Purple Heart

Silver Star

POW Medal

WWII
Victory Medal

American Campaign Medal

Combat Infantryman Badge

Gold Star Banner

Neighborhood Merchants and Services

The commercial areas of the Lithuanian community were near the church and along 10th Street. These businesses included:

Backis Grocery, 711 8th Street – Joseph Backis
Bakery, 8th and Victory
Bakshis Brothers Meats and Groceries, 1002 8th Street – John Bakshis
Dickshot's Dugout, 9th and Victory – Johnny Dickshot
Jakaitis' IGA, 22nd Street in North Chicago
Lincoln Drug, 831 8th Street – Frank Sestokas
S & V Lithuanian Co-op Grocery & Meat Market, 901 8th Street – Tony Servilas
Shaulis Bakery, 810 10th Street
S & J Tailor, 922 10th Street – Stanley Juzamitis

There were also several other taverns in the neighborhood including one owned by the Masilionis family. Other establishments included a barber shop across the street from the drug store, a shoe store across the street from Bakshis' grocery store and a notions store across from the church.

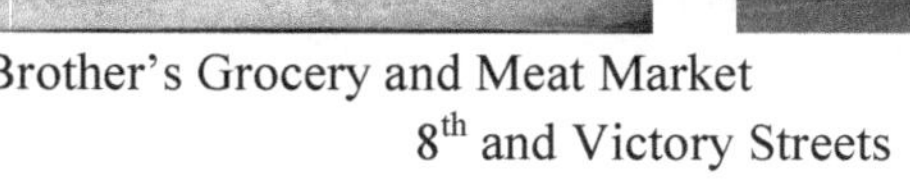

Bakshis Brother's Grocery and Meat Market   Bakery
8th and Victory Streets

Lincoln Drugs
8th and Lincoln Streets

Dickshot's Dugout Tavern
9th and Victory Street

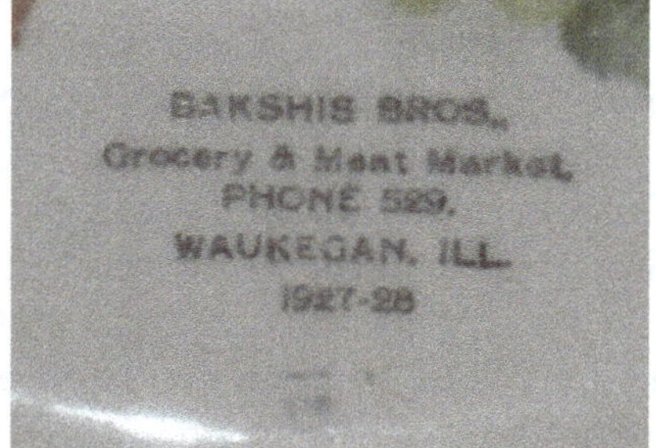

Bakshis Bros. Grocery & Meat Market
9-inch Dinner Plate Premium Offered 1927-28

Petroshius Funeral Home
313 10th Street / North Chicago[54]

---

[54] "© Augustinas Zemaitis - http://global.truelithuania.com"

Fr. Čužauskas, in 1946 listed these parishioners that offered service to the community:

Professionals: Dr. D. Kweder and Dr. J. Zekas.

Pharmacists: Pranas Šeštokas and Edvardas Jankauskas.

Nurses: Viktorija Zupkiūtė-Andrulienė, Cecilija Jonačiūtė-Dargienė, Josephine Zaborskiūtė, Genovaite Zaborskiūtė, Elconora Pavilioniūtė-Decker, Ona Kundrotaitė, Martha Savakiniūtė, Stumbrūtė and Lueija Sutkūtė-Lewis.

Notable Personalities: A.J. Sutkus, real estate business, employee associations, and politician; M. Gust, Internal Revenue Deputy Collector: J. Petroshius, funeral director; W. Skyrius, salesman and parish supporter; Antanas Urban, alderman; J. Matulėnas, Supervisor Assistant; J. Butkus, Precinct Captain; P. Bujanauskas, Music and dance teacher, and works with his wife; Michalina Zaveskienė, active in associations and a prolific writer; J. Bukangtis, a diligent worker of the press at the newspaper; J. Jakutis, a remarkable speaker; Vitus Rayunas, a great musician and dancer and choir tenor; Aleksas Jankauskas, a friendly worker; J. Leskis, no longer a member of the parish committee. He did a lot of work for the church picnic and bazar.

Since 1946 church societies and social organizations continued to serve the St. Bartholomew community.

In 1969 St. Ann's Society was headed by Ann Butkus, the St. Therese Altar Society had Rita Leonaitis as president, the

Mother's Club which supported the school was headed by Peggy Gupton and the Men's Society's president was Larry Sedar.

Notable among the Lithuanian American Community of Lake County have been long-time members: Gediminas Damasius, Sigita Damasius, Palmira Janusoniene–Westholm, Stasys Milasius, Regina Narusiene, Violeta Rutkauskiene, Elena Remigijus Suziedelis, Eduardas Skališius, Elena Skališienė, and Semigijus Suziedelis.

PAST SAINT BARTHOLOMEW CHURCH CHOIRS

PAST SAINT BARTHOLOMEW CHURCH CHOIRS

St. Bartholomew Church Chorus
Circa 1979

St. Bartholomew Church Chorus

St. Bartholomew's Parishioners - 1946

Notable personalities and prominent members of the community are always of interest, but communities are made up of many anonymous individuals. Fr. Čužauskas' 1946 history of the parish included rosters of parishioners and their weekly contributions to the church and their donations supporting the building of the new church. There was no privacy for contributors. Fr. Čužauskas posted names and dollar amounts for every donor to the parish. Fr. Čužauskas' only nod to confidentiality was the fact that his lists showed only the donors initials. Basically, neighbors could see how they stacked up with their neighbors in their support of the church.

Sunday donations were given by 459 parishioners or families. In 1946 they donated a total of $13,746, and averaged $29.88 per year ($0.57 per week) per family. The median contribution was $24.50 per family. In 2017 dollars this amounted to $180,952 total and an average of $3,480 per week.

Contributions for the new church totaled $38,087 with an average of $137.50 per contributor. In 2017 dollars this amounted to $520,734 total with an average of $1,080 per contributor. Considering the fact that donations were being collected at the height of the great depression, one should marvel at the generosity and commitment of the parish members.

Fr. Čužauskas' rosters illustrate the size of the Lithuanian community. These families and individuals were committed to their community and the Catholic Church by providing financial support to the church and participating in parish activities. They were the heart and soul of the Lithuanian community. These are the families that made up the parish of St. Bartholomew:

Abel, M.
Adamski, F. & M.
Aidikonis, M. & M.
Aidikonis, S.
Aidikonis, S. & V.
Aikus, A. & M.
Aikus, F. & A.
Aikus, J.
Aikus, M.
Aikus, S. & K.
Akramas, J. & T
Akuseviciene, M.
Alekna, F.
Aleksionis, Z. & J.
Alksnis, A.
Alksnis, A.
Alksnis, B.
Ambroziunas, C. & F.
Andrulis, J.
Andrulis, V.
Ashmus, F. & E.
Asmiene, V.
August, G. & P.
Augustavičius, J. P.
Augustavičius, S. & A.

Austinas, S. & A.
Auziene, M.
Auzis, A. & M.

Backys, J. & A. Jr.
Backys, J. & A. Jr.
Backys, J. & A. Sr.
Backys, J. & M.
Bagden, C.
Bagdonas, A.
Bagdonas, B.
Bagdonas, C. & L.
Bagdonas, C. & S.
Bagdonas, P.
Bagdonas, S.
Bagdonas, T.
Bakshis, F. & A.
Bakshis, J. & A.
Bakshis, J. & S.
Bakshis, N.
Banis, A. & A.
Banis, P.
Banis, P. & P.
Baron, F. & B.
Baronas, C. & A.

Baronas, F. & A.
Baronas, G.
Baronas, T.
Bastys, F. & P.
Bennett, J.
Bernotas, A. & J.
Biliauskas, V. & A.
Bioletto, P. & B.
Blanchard, A.
Bokas, F. & A.
Brown, T.
Buitkus, J. & M.
Bujanauskas, F. & M.
Bukaas, B.
Bukantis, A. & J.
Bukantis, G. Sr.
Bukantis, J. & A.
Bukantis, P. & M.
Bukantis, W. B.
Bukas, J. & J.
Buksas, A. & V.
Buksas, F. & M.
Buksas, J.
Buksas, J. & M.
Buksas, V. & S.
Burba, A. & V.
Burba, D.
Burba, F.
Burba, F. & C.

Burba, G.
Burba, I. & M.
Butkus, A. & A.
Butkus, A. & G.
Butkus, A. & P.
Butkus, G. & S.
Butkus, J. & A.
Butkus, J. & H.
Butkus, M. & H.
Butkus, R.
Butkus, S.
Butkus, U.
Buzy, A. J.
Buzas, A.

Ceikauskas, S. & A.
Cepaitis, B. & E.
Cepaitis, C. & P.
Chapas, V.
Chapas, V. & A.
Chesney, M.

Dabasinskas, G.
Dabasinskas, M.
Dabasinskas, P.
Dagis, C. & C.
Dagis, K. & A.
Damulis, A.
Daniunas, S. & S.

Gudziunas, S.
Gudzius, P. & A.
Gust, A. & T.
Gust, F.
Gust, M. & V.

Hagen, B.
Hancox, A.
Horen, D.
Hutchings, H.

Jackett, J.
Jakaitis, A. & P.
Jakaitis, H.
Jakaitis, M.
Jakaitis, V &. A.
Jakaitis, V. & D.
Jakaitis, V. & M.
Jakas, A. & B.
Jankauskas, A. & A.
Jankauskas, T.
Janulis, A.
Jarusaitis, K.
Jasukaitis, F. & M.
Jereb, V. & W.
Jocius, J.
Jonaitis, A. & A.
Jonaitis, A. & S.
Jonaitis, A.
Jonaitis, C.

Jonaitis, F. & A.
Jonaitis, H.
Jonaitis, R.
Jonikis, J.
Juncer, A. & B.
Juncer, J. & M.
Junevičius, M.
Jurgaitis, C. & T.
Jurgaitis, P. & B.
Junevičius, A. & M.
Jurgaitis, P. & L.

Kachinskas, E.
Kachinskas, J. & J.
Kairatis, A.
Kairaitis, S.
Kaminskas, A. & V.
Kaminskas, V. & A.
Kanaverskis, P. & U.
Kantautas, G. & A.
Kantautas, M.
Kapter, E.
Karasauskas, T. & G.
Karpis, A.
Kasile, M.
Kasile, S.
Kasper, J. & M.
Kasper, M.
Kazdelevicia, F.
Kibart, A. & M.

Kimbrough, V.
Kisionis, C. & F.
Kiskis, A. & M.
Kliora, C. & F.
Kliora, G. & P.
Kondrad, A.
Kovarsky, S. & A.
Krapf, G. & U.
Krekis, A. & U.
Krist, A. & V.
Kryzius, J.
Kubaitis, V. & A.
Kumickus, F.
Kundrot, A.
Kundrot, J. & J.
Kundrot, S. & S.
Kuzinskas, J. & A.
Kuzmickus, A. & H.
Kuzmickus, A.
Kuzmickus, F. & A.
Kuzmickus, G. & D.
Kuzmickus, J. & E.
Kuzmickus, J. & M.
Kuzmickus, P.
Kweder, M.

Latvaitis, A.
Latvaitis, F.
Latvaitis, G.

Latvaitis, Jos.
Lauraitis, J. & I.
Leonaitis, H.
Leonaitis, P. & G.
Leonavicia, F. & K.
Leonowitz, A.
Leskis, J. & A.
Leskis, P. & D.
Lickus, F. & D.
Likus, C. & I.
Liskus, C.
Liudas, A. & M.
Liudas, I. & E.
Liutvin, J. & J.
Liutvinas, A.
Lukosius E.
Lulis, S.
Lulis, V. & A.
Lushas, J. & B.
Lutvin, G.
Lutvin, M. & A.

Maciulis, A.
Maciulis, B.
Malela, J. & U.
Malinauskas, M.
Mantvilas, B.
Mantvilas, J. & M.
Marcinkus, A. & E.

Marcinkus, A.
Marcinkus, F. & M.
Margis, F. & M.
Marozas, J.
Martinaitis, M. & Z.
Martinaitis, V.
Martynaitis, Z.
Masotas, T. & A.
Matulenas, J. & A.
Matulenas, J. & J.
Matulenas, T.
Mazaitis, P. & E.
Mazrimas, N.
McMahon, A.
Meitzfield, D. I.
Mesec, S. & P.
Mickunas, M. & A.
Mickus, B. & A.
Mickus, E.
Mikalauskas, A.
Mikalauskas, K.
Mikolaitis, A.
Mileska, L. & J.
Mileskas, I. & R.
Morris, M.
Motekaitis, F.
Motekaitis, M.
Motiejaitis, J. & M.
Mugerditchian, J.

Nagode, F. & B.
Naujokas, B.
Naujokas, F. &M.
Naujokas, G.
Naujokas, V.
Navard, C. & A.
Navickas, A.
Navickas, C. & M.
Navickas, J.
Navickas, M.
Nevardauskas, P. & M.
Niemi, P.
Noreikis, C. & M.
Norkus, J.
Norkus, P.

Padora, J.
Paldauskas, J.
Palickis, A.
Palucius, M.
Paluckis, C.
Paluckis, P.
Paluckis, S.
Paluska, H.
Paluska, L. & A.
Paskauskas, A.
Paskauskas, A.
Paskauskas, F.
Paskauskas, V.
Patterson, M.

Pavilionis, C. & P.
Pazereskis, P.
Pazereskis, S. & F.
Peters, C. & A.
Petkus, A. & I.
Petkus, C. & A.
Petkus, J. & J.
Petkus, K. & S.
Petkus, P.
Petraitis, G. & S.
Petraitis, J. & B.
Petroshius, J. & A.
Petruska, C. & J.
Petruska, C. & M.
Petruska, F. & A.
Petruska, F. & H.
Petruska, F.
Petruska, G. & A.
Petruska, H.
Petruska, J. & E.
Petruska, J.
Petruska, J. & M.
Petruska, M. & V.
Petruska, S. & F.
Petruska, S. & M.
Petruska, V.
Pipeius, A. & H.
Plutkas, C. & J.
Plutkis, A.

Plutkis, S.
Pocius, J. & C.
Pocius, J. & J.
Pocius, J. & K.
Pocius, P. & M.
Pojunas, J.
Pojunas, T.
Ponzio, A. & B.
Povilaitis, F.
Povilaitis, V.

Racas, G.
Racas, J.
Racas, V. & A.
Raila, J.
Rainis, U.
Rakauskas, M. & M.
Rauda, F.
Raudonis, J.
Raudonis, K.
Rayunas, A. & A.
Rayunas, B.
Rayunas, F. & D.
Rayunas, P. & F.
Rayunas, S. & S.
Rayunas, V. & F.
Rayunas, V. & S.
Remaikis, A.
Remaikis, P.

Rimkus, U.
Rukas, C.
Rumsa, F. & A.
Rumsa, H.
Rumsa, L.
Rūta, M.
Rutell, E. & M.
Rutell, M.
Rybikauskas, M.

Sacevičius, E.
Sadauskas, A.
Sadauskas, F. & A.
Sadauskas, J. & C.
Salata, S. & J.
Salcius, E.
Salcius, J.
Salcius, M.
Salucka, A.
Samuelian, G.
Savage, B.
Sawakin, B. & L.
Schapalas, S. & I.
Schapals, B.
Schapals, S.
Sedar, F. & E.
Sedar, L. & L.
Sereikis, G.
Sestokas, F.
Shaulis, H.

Shaulis, P. & R.
Shaulis, U.
Shaulis, V.
Shimkus, R.
Shimulinas, J. & J.
Shimulinas, J.
Siaulis, M. & A.
Sidlauskas, J.
Sidlauskas, P. & V.
Sidlauskas, V. & A.
Simkus, R.
Sirvydas, B. & J.
Skarbalis, A.
Skyrius, E.
Skyrius, W.
Slazas, M.
Slazas, U.
Smith, K. & A.
Smith, M.
Snaukstas, B. & A.
Spokas, W. & E.
Stanulis, T. & A.
Steponkus, A. & A.
Streed, B.
Stulginskas, C. & E.
Stulginskas, F. & A.
Stulginskas, M. & M.
Stumbris, G. & V.
Sukaitis, A.
Sukaitis, J. & P.

Sutinis, B.
Sutinis, S.
Sutkus, A. & J.
Sutkus, F.
Svambaris, T. & E.
Svazas, C. & E.
Svytorius, F. & S.
Svytorius, V. & M.
Sweda, B. & S.

Tauchs, A. & F.
Thalke, M.
Todd, J.
Treinauskas, V. & K.
Trust, A. & R.
Trust, F. & M.
Turauskas, F. & A.
Turauskiene, A.
Turcinskaite, K.
Turcinskas, J. & J.

Unewitz, J. & A.
Urbaites, P. & M.
Urbaitis, J. & S.
Urban, A.
Urban, L.
Urban, V.
Urbick, P. & T.
Urbonas, A.

Urbonas, S. & A.
Urman, T. & A.
Urmonas, G. & T.
Uzemeckis, A. & D.

Vaisnoras, P.
Vaitekūnas, A.
Vaitekūnas, C. & A.
Vaitekūnas, J. & A.
Vaitekūnas, K. & P.
Valilius A.
Valis, U.
Vandermark, A.
VanderVere, E. & A.
Vardauskas, A. Jr.
Vardauskas, J. & A.
Vasilius, A. & A.
Vasilius, A.
Vasilius, C. & H.
Vasilius, M.
Vasilius, V. & E.
Venclauskas, V. & K.
Verpecinskas, C. & A.
Vincevičius, J. & M.
Virakas, J. & F.
Vizgerd, S.

Wagner, W.
Walczak, C. & S.

Weiss, S.
Wells, W. & A.
Yoknis, C. & A.
Yoknis, M.

Zaborskis, J. & A.
Zakarauskas, A. & E.
Zakas, I. & B.
Zaugra, A.
Zaugra, F. & E.
Zavaski, G. & M.
Zavaski, J.
Zekas, Dr. J. & M.
Zylius, S. & A.

Zekas, J. & Z.
Zekonis, A. & M.
Zevaski, P. & F.
Ziaugra, F. & E.
Zickus, J. & M.
Zigas, D.
Zigas, L & A.
Zilaitis, J. & V.
Ziuraitis, J. & R.
Zupan, J. & B.
Zupkus, V. & A.
Zupansic, A.

St. Bartholomew's Priests and Nuns

Priests:

1893	Fr. Jurgis Kolesinskas	
1893	Fr. Matas Krauciunas	Services twice per month
1896-1901	Fr. Edvardus Steponavičius	Part-time
1901-1904	Fr. Matas Smolenskas	First Full-time Resident Pastor
1904	Fr. Vincas Girdžiūnas	Assistant priest
1904-1905	Fr. Kazimieras Ambrozaitis	Pastor
1905	No Pastor	
1906-1909	Fr. Juozas Stočkus	Pastor
1909-1913	Fr. Mykolas Krušas	Pastor
1913-1918	Fr. Konstantinas Zaikauskas	Pastor
1918	Fr. F. Meškauskas	Assistant priest
1918	Fr. Pranas Būčys	Assistant priest – Marian fathers
1918-1931	Fr. Jonas B. Kloris	Pastor
1931-1955	Fr. Juosas J. Čužauskas	Pastor
1934-39	Fr. Walter Urba	Assistant priest
1940's	Fr. Alban Kishkunas	Assistant priest
1940's	Fr. Anastasius Valančius	Assistant priest
1955-1974	Fr. Stanley Jonelis	Pastor
1960's-70's	Fr. Zigmund Romanauskas	Assistant Priest
1974-1979	Fr John A. Kuzinskas	Pastor / Parish Administrator 1973-74
1979-1991	Fr. William Zavaski	Pastor

Nuns:

St. Bartholomew School was established 1912, and relinquished May 31, 1989. The opening date for St. Bartholomew School was September 20, 1912. Two hundred seventy-five students were enrolled. There were four classrooms with grades one through six. From the years 1934 until the school closed, 129 Sisters of St. Casimir taught students at St. Bartholomew School.

Mother Maria Kaupus
1912-1913
Sr. Anita, Sup. 1950-51
Sr. Ann Barbara 1985-87
Sr. Jo Therese 1971-72
Sr. M. Adele 1954-55
Sr. M. Adrian 1971-72
Sr. M. Agnetta 1954-56
Sr. M. Alfreda 1937-39
1949-1951
Sr. M. Aloiza, Sup. 1921
Sr. M. Alvira 1974-75
Sr. M. Amedea 1942-43
Sr. M. Andrea 1980-81
Sr. M. Angela, Sup. 1918
Sr. M. Aniceta 1948-49
Sr. M. Anita, 1934-35,
Sup. 1949-52
Sr. M. Anthony 1967-68
Sr. M. Anysia 1957-58, 1960-
61, 1963-64
Sr. M. Aquina 1943-44,
1945-47
Sr. M. Augustine 1945-46

Sr. M. Aurelia 1968-71
Sr. M. Aureline 1936-40
Sr. M. Barbara 1946-47
Sr. M. Bartholomew
1955-56
Sr. M. Benigna 1964-65
Sr. M. Bertilia 1943-44,
1966-67
Sr. M. Bonaventura,
1912-1913,
Sup. 1924
Sr. M. Brunona 1958-61
Sr. M. Celine 1974-80,
Sup. 1980-83
Sr. M. Celita 1947-48
Sr. M. Charles 1952-53
Sr. M. Christella 1983-84
Sr. M. Christopher
1947-48
Sr. M. Clemencia 1947-48
Sr. M. Clemense 1961-62
Sr. M. Clotilda 1939-1940
Sr. M. Coletta 1950-53

Sr. M. Conrad,
    Sup 1943-46, 1973-74
Sr. M. Consumata 1944-45
Sr. M. Cordia 1958-59
Sr. M. Cordis 1946-47
Sr. M. Cunegunda
    1952-53
Sr. M. David 1974-75
Sr. M. Deborah 1963-65
Sr. M. Delphine,
    Sup. 1983-84
Sr. M. Dolora,
    Sup. 1954-60
Sr. M. Dolorosa,
    Sup. 1915
Sr. M. Edwarda 1936-40,
    Sup. 1963-1971
Sr. M. Edwina 1935-36
Sr. M. Elalia 1938-39
Sr. M. Elizabeth 1951-54,
    1983-1985
Sr. M. Elizbieta,
    Sup. 1916, 1923
Sr. M. Emiliana 1948-49
Sr. M. Eulalia 1936-38
Sr. M. Eulogia 1959-60
Sr. M. Falicita 1944-45
Sr. M. Fedelia, Sup. 1922
Sr. M. Gemma 1988-89
Sr. M. Generosa 1961-63
Sr. M. Genovaite,
    Sup. 1919-1920
Sr. M. Georgine,
    Sup. 1960-63
Sr. M. Geraldine 1951-52

Sr. M. Gertrude,
    Sup. 1946-49
    Sup. 1952-54
Sr. M. Goretti 1954-55
Sr. M. Gracilda 1945-47
Sr. M. Hiacinta,
    Sup. 1929-1934
Sr. M. Ignatia 1977-78
Sr. M. Innocenta,
    Sup. 1940-43
Sr. M. Inviolata 1953-54,
    1967-69, 1986-88
    (Anne Baubin)
Sr. M. Jacob 1946-48
Sr. M. Jeanette 1947-53
Sr. M. Joanita 1935-36
Sr. M. Josanne 1966-67
Sr. M. Joselle 1962-63
Sr. M. Josita 1948-50
Sr. M. Julia 1941-43,
    1945-46
Sr. M. Justina, Sup. 1917
Sr. M. Kazimiera
    1912-1913
Sr. M. Kathleen 1962-63
Sr. M. Laurita 1936-37
Sr. M. Leona 1947-48
Sr. M. Lilian 1973-74
Sr. M. Liliosa 1971-72,
    Sup. 1972-73
Sr. M. Lillian 1940-41
Sr. M. Marietta 1951-52
Sr. M. Marionette
    1983-84. 1985-86
Sr. M. Marissa 1963-67

Sr. M. Martina 1944-45

Sr. M. Maurita 1958-59

Sr. M. Mechtilde 1934-36

Sr. M. Melania 1953-55,
1959-1961

Sr. M. Michael 1972-74

Sr. M. Michaeline
1955-56

Sr. M. Michele 1956-58,
1961-62

Sr. M. Natalija 1912-1913

Sr. M. Nathaniel 1956-58

Sr. M. Nichola 1939-1941,
1972-73

Sr. M. Norbert 1949-50,
1953-54

Sr. M. Patrice 1953-55

Sr. M. Pauletta 1943-45

Sr. M. Petrita 1953-56

Sr. M. Priscilla 1950-51

Sr. M. Raymond 1940-41

Sr. M. Remigia 1959-60

Sr. M. Reparta 1934-36

Sr. M. Rosalia 1948-49,
1969-89

Sr. M. Rosita 1967-68

Sr. M. Ruth 1940-43

Sr. M. Salome
Sup. 1925-1928

Sr. M. Seraphina 1934-36,
1967-72

Sr. M. Simeon 1965-66

Sr. M. Sylviana 1956-57

Sr. M. Thecla 1956-59

Sr. M. Theodata 1958-59

Sr. M. Theodore 1949-51

Sr. M. Theophane
1942-44, 1955-56

Sr. M. Theresine 1975-83

Sr. M. Thomas 1941-42

Sr. M. Thomasanne
1965-66

Sr. M. Thomasita 1959-64

Sr. M. Vita, Sup 1971-72

Sr. M. Viventia 1955-58,
1969-70

Sr. M. Wanda Marie
1970-71, 1984-85

Sr. M. Winifred
Sup. 1934-40

Sr. M. Theophane
1941-42

Sr. Magdalen Bagdonas
Sup. 1974-80,
1980-83

Sr. Maria Alphonsa
1972-74

Sr. Marionette 1984-85

Sr. Pauline Bogan 1970-71

Sr. Ruth Ambrose
1985-87

Seal of the Sisters of St. Casimir

St. Bartholomew alumna Marilyn Kuzmickus became the seventh General Superior of the Sisters of St. Casimir in 1988. She served in this capacity for ten years - until 1998. During her tenure Sister Kuzmickus faced the challenge of diminishing numbers of Sisters and the closing schools. Many Sisters were retiring from full time work, and fewer members were entering the order. Emphasis was given to mission effectiveness.

> Under Sister Marilyn's direction a Board of Directors composed of religious and lay was initiated at St. Joseph Home and also at Villa Joseph Marie High School in Holland, PA. The President / Principal model was initiated at Maria High School, the first Catholic girls' high school within the Chicago Archdiocese to assume this type of leadership. Representing the two Sisters of St. Casimir hospitals, Holly Cross and Loretto, Sister Marilyn played an active role along with other major superiors in efforts to unite and

strengthen the position of Catholic healthcare within the Archdiocese of Chicago.[55]

Sister Kuzmickus also became the first Archdiocesan Postulator for the Beatification Cause of Mother Maria.

Sister Marilyn Kuzmickus   With Pope John Paul II
General Superior of the Sisters of St. Casimir
1988-1998

The influence of the Sisters of St. Casimir can be seen in the number of their students who became nuns or priests. In total, 16 women and 15 men from the community found vocations in the religious life.

---

[55] Sisters of St. Casimir – A Journey in Faith – 100 Years 1907-2007; Booklink, Ireland copyright 2007 page 55

VOCATIONS TO THE RELIGIOUS LIFE

WERE FULFILLED BY

THESE SISTERS FROM OUR PARISH

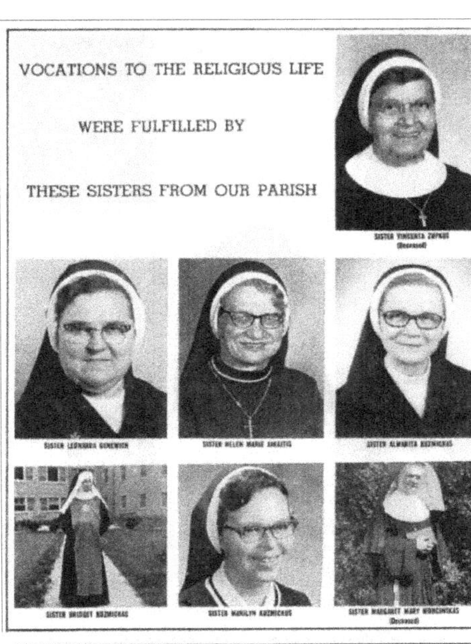

SISTER VINCENTA ZUPKUS
(Deceased)

SISTER LEONARDA GUNEWICH
SISTER HELEN MARIE ANKAITIS
SISTER ALMARITA KUZMICKAS

SISTER BRIDGET KUZMICKAS
SISTER MARILYN KUZMICKAS
SISTER MARGARET MARY WORCINSKAS
(Deceased)

SISTER ADOLPHINE NAVARO
SISTER IGNATIA PETRUSKA
SISTER MARLENE PETRUSKA

SISTER THOMASETTE SCHEELEN
SISTER BAPTISTA SCIGLINSKAITE
(Deceased)
SISTER ANNE MARIE NAKARTHAS

SISTER SERAPHINA VESALGA
(Deceased)
SISTER BERNICE KALIS-WALLIS
SISTER GABRIEL WINSLOW

Reverend Joseph Gilbert

Reverend Wesław Zbrisk

Reverend Robert Brazauskas, O. Carm.

Reverend Robert Backis

Brother Albert A. Sutkus, S.M.

Reverend Bart Juncer

Reverend John Kuzinskas

Fr Antanas Matulenas - OSB

Reverend Mike Nacius

Reverend Brian Paulson, S.J.
Midwest Provincial – S.J.
St. Anastasia

Reverend Stanislaus Petrauskas

Fr. Simon Rakauskas, OSB

Not pictured
Fr. Raymond Matulenas, OSB
Fr. J. Pakauskas
Fr. John Shaulis

In 1970 Archbiship Paul Marchinkus accompanied Pope Paul VI on tour of the Phillippines. During this visit the Pope was attacked by a knife-weilding assailant.

> Luckily for Pope Paul VI, his friend and Chicago native Archbishop Paul Marcinkus – a burly, 6'4" man – was nearby and tackled the would-be assassin, saving the pontiff's life. In thanks for Marcinkus' quck thinking and actions, Paul VI gave him a chalice the pope used while ordaining priests during the visit.
>
> The chalice has a personal inscription on the bottom: "Chalice used by Pope Paul VI in ordination in Manila November 28, 1970. Gift of Pope Paul VI to Paul C. Marcinkus." Paul VI's seal is embedded in the center.
>
> Thanks to Auxiliary Bishop George Rassas and the Sisters of St. Casimir, the chalice is now in the care of the University of St. Mary of the Lake/Mundelein Seminary and will be used for special celebrations and liturgies.[56]

At some point Archbishop Marcincus gifted the chalice to his good friend Msgr. John Kuzinskis. Msgr. Kuzinskis in turn gifted the chalice to the Sisters of St. Casimir. Both Marinkus and Kuzinskis had been taught by the Sisters of St. Cazimir while in grade school – Marcinkus at St. Anthony in Cicero, IL and Kuzinskis at St. Bartholomew

---

[56] Chalice related to assassination attempt on Paul VI finds home at Mundelein. Chicago Catholic - Newspaper of the Archdiocese of Chicago. July 18, 2017

in Waukegan.[57]   While Archbishop Marchincus was not from Lake County, Lake County Lithuanians should take pride in the fact that this chalice now resides in the middle of a vibrant Lithuanian community.

Archbishop Paul Marcinkus

Pope Paul VI
Chalice

Chalice Inscription
" Gift of Pope Paul VI
To
Paul C Marcinkus"

---

[57] Sisters of St. Casimir Donate Chalice to Mundelein Seminary. "Journeys". Sisters of St. Casimir Vol XXXI No. 2. Pall 2017 p.6

Lithuanian Hall

The St. Bartholomew Society along with the St. Joseph's Society built a meeting hall in 1909. The hall served as a social center for the community. By 1926 the original was too small to meet the needs of the community. The original building was replaced by a new, larger building. The new Lithuanian Auditorium was opened in 1929 at 901 South Lincoln Street. Lithuanian Hall or "Lugan Hall", as it was generally called, hosted plays, concerts, wedding receptions, meetings and hosted the offices of the Lithuanian Building and Loan Association.

Play

Choir

Circa 1915

St. Joseph's Society Pin
Circa 1897

A highlight of the year was an annual Christmas party at the Lithuanian Hall for all the children of the community. The party was a joint effort of the St. Bartholomew Society, the St Joseph Society, and the St. Anthony Society. The party featured a visit from Santa Claus, games and presents. Memories of the party are vivid in the minds of those who attended.

> Oh my goodness. We lived a block away and went to many wedding receptions there. Also events like the Lithuanian dancers. Our school Christmas party put on by the men's club was there too. The whole school would march over from the school to "Lugan Hall" singing Christmas songs.[58]

The Lithuanian Society often sponsored dances on Saturday night. In addition to local bands, the Hall would feature "big name" bands such as Frankie Yankovic. Many young people attended, met, fell in love and got married as a result of these social gatherings.

On February 16th there were large annual celebrations of the 1918 restoration of Lithuanian statehood.

Wedding receptions in the Hall had a standard menu: fried chicken, ham, Lithuanian sausage, mashed potatoes, and sauerkraut. All these were served family-style. Entertainment was provided by a local polka band.

---

[58] Correspondence with Mary Novak-Zupec, 2017

Lithuanian Hall[59]
901 South Lincoln Street

The Lithuanian Auditorium issued trade tokens for use in the community.

> . . . trade tokens are "good for" tokens, issued by merchants. Generally, they have a merchant's name or initials, sometimes a town and state, and a value legend (such as "good for 5¢" or other denomination) somewhere on the token. Types of merchants that issued tokens included general stores, grocers, department stores, dairies, meat markets, drug stores, saloons, bars, taverns, barbers, coal mines, lumber mills and many other businesses. The era of 1870 through 1920 marked the highest use of "trade tokens" in the United States, spurred by the proliferation of small stores in rural areas. Thousands of small general and merchandise stores were to be found all over the United States and many of them used trade tokens

---

[59] "© Augustinas Zemaitis - http://global.truelithuania.com"

to promote trade and extend credit to customers. Aluminum tokens almost always date after 1890, when low-cost production began.[60]

Lithuanian Hall Merchant's Tokens
Circa 1920s

About 1985 the Lithuanian Hall building was sold and now serves the Hispanic community as Hacienda del Norte.

---

[60] (Wikipedia https://en.wikipedia.org/wiki/Token_coin)

Lithuanian Language

In the early 1800's Lithuanians under Russian rule began a movement to re-establish their right to sovereignty. In the 1860's the Russian government suppressed the Lithuanian language. Lithuanian books and newspapers were banned and schools were forbidden to use the Lithuanian language. The Lithuanian language was seen as one piece of evidence that Lithuania was once, and should again be an independent nation. Linguists pointed to connections between the Lithuanian language and ancient Sanskrit. The claim has been made that Lithuanian is the oldest language in the Indo-European language group.   Fr. Čužauskas included several examples of the links in his history of St. Bartholomew Church: [61]

English	Lithuanian	Sanskrit
What	kas	kas
God	Dievas	Deva
Son	sūnus	sunu
Daughter	duktė	duhita
Brother	brolis	bhrat
Eye	akis	akshi
Nose	nosis	nasa
Night	naktis	nakta
Water	vanduo	unduo

---

[61] Juozis Cuzaukas, Nusekę Antplūdžiai Waukegan'o Lietuvių Istorija, page 67

English	Lithuanian	Sanskrit
Fire	ugnis	agnis
Honey	medus	madhu
One	vienas	eka
Two	du	dvi
Three	trys	tri
Four	keturi	cetur
Five	penki	pancan
Six	šeši	shash
Seven	septyni	sapton
Eight	aštuoni	ashton
Nine	devyni	navan
Ten	dešimtas	dason

Some useful Lithuanian phrases are:

Hello	Labas
How are you?	Kaip tau einus
Good	Gerai
Very good	Laba gerai
Please	Prašom
Thank you	Ačiū
Thank you very much	Ačiū labai
Yes	Taip
No	Ne

Good morning	Labas rytas
Good afternoon	Laba diena
Good evening	Laba varkara
Good night	Labanaktis

Water	Vanduo
Tea	Arbata
Beer	Alus

Merry Christmas	Linksmų Kalėdų
Happy New Year	Laimingų naujųjų metų
Happy Easter	Su Velykomis
Happy Birthday	Su gimtadieniu

From the sample phrases given above the reader should note that the Lithuanian alphabet consists of 33 characters:[62]

Aa Ąą Bb Cc Čč Dd Ee Ęę Ėė Ff Gg Hh Ii Įį Yy Jj
Kk Ll Mm Nn Oo Pp Rr Ss Šš Tt Uu Ųų Ūū Zz Žž

Unique pronunciations for Lithuanian are as follows:

Ąą	sounds like the *a* in *father*
Čč	similar the *ch* sound in *church*
Ęę	like the *a* in *bad*
Ėė	similar to the *a* in *made*

---

[62] Leonardas Dambriunas, Antanas Klimas, William R. Schmalstieg. Introduction
to Modern Lithuanian. Franciscan Fathers, Brooklyn, NY 1972 pages 4-17

Įį	like *ee* in *keel*
Šš	similar to the *sh* sound in *sheep*
Ųų	like the *u* in *truth*
Ūū	also sounds like the *u* in *truth*
Žž	like *sure* in measure or *ge* in rouge

An interesting note about Lithuanian surnames. There are distinctions made regarding females place within the family. Female surnames differ depending on the woman's marital status. Unmarried women's surnames end in either –itė or –ytė - whereas married women's surnames end in –ienė.

For example:
    Benedict Truskauskas is the husband
    Anna Galinauskitė-Truskauskienė is his wife
    Sons are Truskauskas
    Daughters are Truskauskaitė.

Another example:
    Jonas Bakšys is the husband
    Sophie Truskauskaitė-Bakšienė is his wife
    Sons are Bakšys
    Daughters are Bakšytė

Throughout this book Lithuanian surnames have been written using both English and Lithuanian spellings interchangeably. The choice was made to incorporate the spelling used in the source documents for the entry.

Common among ethnic neighborhoods is the use of their native language at home and around the neighborhood. Immigrants generally use their native language at home and when necessary they use English at work. When the immigrant group is large and centrally located the native language can be used outside the home. In fact, with large communities the native language may be the only language that one would need to know. With ethnic stores and services one could conceivable live their entire life without having to learn English. Many of St. Bartholomew's early students spoke only Lithuanian at the time they entered school. The Sisters of St. Casimir had to teach not only reading, writing and arithmetic but they also had to teach their students basic English.

By the 1950's the opposite was true. The third and fourth generation students had little or no fluency with the Lithuanian language. Under the guidance of the Sister of St. Casimir these students received one hour per week instruction in the Lithuanian language.

When Fr. Bill Zavaski, a St. Bart's alum, assumed the position of pastor in April, 1979 he was informed that masses needed to be offered in Lithuanian, English and Spanish. As a third-generation Lithuanian his language skills needed improvement, so he hired a tutor, Stella Tamasauskas,

> By June he was able to say Mass in Lithuanian and
> by Christmas he had progressed to the point where
> he was able to deliver his first sermon – "my gift to
> the parishioners," he said.

He wrote the sermon in English and his tutor's son, Al Tamasauskas, who is educated in theology, translated it for him. "It is a very difficult language," Father Zavaski said. Reputed to be the oldest language in Europe, its roots are in Sanskrit.[63]

Under Fr. Zavaski's leadership, classes were organized to teach the Lithuanian language and traditions to the community.

The Lithuanian language serves as both a source of unity and a source of division within the Lithuanian community. First- and second-generation Lithuanians generally have excellent language skills that the third-generation and later do not possess. If inclusion in the Lithuanian community is defined by DNA, then all generations are "Lithuanian". If linguistic fluency in the litmus test, then the third-generation and later descendants could quickly be eliminated. This is an issue that the Lithuanian American Community needs to address.

---

[63] Waukegan News Sun 1980

Lithuanian Food

Lithuanian food has been described as "indicative of the arduous times endured by the people during invasions, wars, and several occupations by neighbors. The more lavish foods became favorites during periods of national affluence, particularly during its independence between the two great wars."[64]

Arguably the closest thing to a Lithuanian national dish is kugelis. Given twenty women one would probably get 30 or more different recipes for the dish. Here are a few recipes:

Potato Pudding (Kugelis) #1[65]

5 lbs. Idaho potatoes
½ - ¾ lb. chopped bacon
1 med. Onion, chopped
1 (6 oz.) can evaporated milk
5 eggs
2 tsp. salt
½ tsp. pepper

Fry bacon. Add onion and continue frying. Grate potatoes. Beat eggs with milk. Add all ingredients to the

---

[64] Walter Oleksy, The old Country Cookbook, Nelson-Hall Company, Chicago, IL 1974 page 103

[65] Pasaulio Lietuviu Centro Moteru Skanumynu Receptai, Skaniai Valgome, PLC, Lemont, IL 1996 page 175

potatoes and mix well. Pour into a 15 x 10 in. greased pan.

Bake in a preheated oven at 350 degrees for 1 ½ hours.

Potato Pudding (Kugelis) #2[66]

4 raw potatoes
2 boiled potatoes
1 egg
1 cup milk
2 tbsps. Bacon fat
1 tbsp. flour
1 tsp. baking powder
Salt, pepper

Peel raw potatoes, grate fine. Mash peeled boiled potatoes. Combine both with remaining ingredients. Pour into greased tin or casserole. Bake at 450 degrees 15 minutes; reduce to 350 degrees, bake 45 minutes longer.

---

[66] Josephine J. Daužvardis, Popular Lithuanian Recipes, Lithuanian Catholic Press Society, Chicago, IL 1971 page107

Potato Pudding (Kugelis) #3[67]

5 large potatoes

1 medium onion
1 stick of butter or margarine
 handful of cream of wheat
1 small can of Carnation evaporated milk
3 eggs
Salt and pepper to taste
1 tablespoon baking powder

Pre-heat oven to 350°.
Dice the onion and sauté in the butter.
Peel potatoes and place in a sauce pan with water. Grate the potatoes and add most of the milk to prevent browning.
Combine eggs and the rest of the milk. Then add them to the mix.
Blend in onion, margarine, cream of wheat, salt, pepper, and baking powder.

Another variation on the recipe is to brown a half pound of bacon and crumble it and some of the grease into the Kugelis for extra flavor.

Bake in a greased 9"x15" cake pan until burned on the edges. Usually 1-1 1/2 hours. I have found that pre-heating the oven to 400° and baking the kugelis for 1/4 hour and then reducing the heat to 350° does a better job of baking.

Serve kugelis with sour cream and salt and more crumbled bacon.

---

[67] Sophie Bakshis family recipe

"Pointers on Making Good Kugelis" are offered by Josephine Daužvardis:

1. Use old Potatoes.
2. Depth of grated potato mixture should be no less than 2 1/2 –inches in baking dish.

3. Start baking at high temperature, then reduce temperature to complete baking.[68]

Potato Pancakes

Potato pancakes are a quick and easy taste delight.

7-8 medium potatoes
2 eggs
3 tbsps. flour
1 tsp. salt

Peel and grate potatoes. Mix in other ingredients. Melt fat or heat 1 tbsp. cooking oil in frying pan. Drop spoons full of mixture into hot fat, fry each side olden grown. Fry golden brown in small amount of hot fat or oil.[69]

Serve with sour cream and salt (fried crumbled bacon optional)

---

[68] Josephine J. Daužvardis, Popular Lithuanian Recipes, Lithuanian Catholic Press Society, Chicago, IL 1971 page 108

[69] Josephine J. Daužvardis, Popular Lithuanian Recipes, Lithuanian Catholic Press   Society, Chicago, IL 1971 page 104

Potato "Zeppelins" – Potato Meat Dumplings

12 large potatoes
3 or 4 boiled potatoes
Salt to taste

MEAT MIXTURE:
½ lb. ground beef
½ lb. ground veal
½ lb. ground pork (optional. If not used, increase other meats by this amount)
1 chopped onion
½ tbsp. shortening (bacon drippings are good)
1 tsp. salt
¼ tsp. pepper
2 eggs

TOPPING OR GRAVY;
½ lb. bacon
1 chopped onion
2 or 3 tbsps. Sour cream (optional)

Grate peeled and washed potatoes. Drain through cheese cloth, straining as dry as possible. Let the strained liquid stand until starch accumulates in bottom of bowl. Pour off the liquid carefully and add the starch to grated potatoes. Grate or mash boiled potatoes and add to grated raw potatoes. Add salt to taste. Mix thoroughly.

In a frying pan sauté the chopped onion in shortening. Add meat, salt and pepper and cook slowly for about half an hour, stirring occasionally. Cool slightly. Add eggs, mixing thoroughly. Left-over ground meats can be used. Just add to sautéed onions and heat through.

Take about a cupful of the potato mixture, pat it flat on the palm of the hand, or on a slightly floured board, to about 1/3 inch thickness. Place a heaping teaspoon of the meat mixture in the center. Fold potato mixture around meat, seal edges firmly. Pat into shape of a large egg. Drop into pot of boiling water to which about a teaspoon of salt has been added. Make certain that water resumes boiling after adding each dumpling. Do not overcrowd dumplings in pot. Stir carefully occasionally. Boil about 25 minutes. Remove from water, drain and place on heated platter.

Dice bacon, fry with onion, pouring off some of excess fat. Sprinkle over dumplings. For a richer gravy stir sour cream carefully into bacon-onion after it has cooled a bit. Blend well - do not boil. Pour over dumplings.[70]

Lithuanian Sausage

Another favorite food was fresh Lithuanian sausage. Never ask how the sausage is made. At Bakshis Brother's Meats and Groceries the recipe was simple: Pitch end pieces and scrap meat into a barrel of brine. When the barrel was full (about once or twice a month) grind everything up and add spices. Then stuff the

---

[70] Josephine J. Daužvardis, Popular Lithuanian Recipes, Lithuanian Catholic Press Society, Chicago, IL 1971 page 110

sausage. Sometimes add extra ham to give the sausage some extra flavor.[71]

Other popular delights were Lithuanian rye bread, Fried Onion Greens, Farmer's cheese, and cucumbers with sour cream.

Lithuanian Rye Bread

Lithuanian rye bread is distinctive for its thick dark crust, robust flavor, and firm texture mixed with caraway seed. In the unlikely chance that a loaf was left on the shelf to long the bread does not develop mold. The loaf is so solid and shelf-stable that one could (jokingly) build a house with it. An interesting note about the bread: In the old country the rye bread was considered a dietary staple and white bread was considered to be a luxury. In America the opposite is the norm.

Fried Onion Greens

Fried onion greens are a nice snack food. Sauté onion greens with diced bacon and serve them with a little salt on a piece of Lithuanian rye bread.

Farmer's Cheese

Farmer's cheese is a firm, dry, dense, white cheese. The cheese is cut into generous slices, buttered and salted.

---

[71] Conversation with John Bakshis - 1982

Cucumbers and Sour Cream

There was a time before Paul Newman and Kraft when people enjoyed salads. For Lithuanians a popular choice was sliced cucumbers in sour cream sprinkled with salt.

In a 1976 conversation with Anna Zemaitis-Bakshis-Chapas (AC – age 72), her cousin Anna Shimulinas-Bakshis (AB - age 82) and Bob Bakshis (BB) they said:

> In the Hell. In the Hell I have a good time with the devil. (AC)
> Dance with the devils. (AB)
> Yeah, Dance with the devils. Eat the cucumbers with the sour cream. (AC laugh)
> What's this? (BB)
> In Europe they used to say how I want to go to hell when I die, I get the cucumbers with the sour cream. (AC laugh)
> They think that the devils eat nothing but the cucumbers with the sour cream. (AB laugh)
> Maybe somebody don't like it so they say like that and start it. (AC laugh) [72]

---

[72] Robert Bakshis, Conversation with Anna Chapas and Anna Bakshis November 29, 1975

Lithuanian Traditions

Faith, Family and Food define the core elements of a community. For the Lithuanian community the holidays of Christmas and Easter are illustrative.

Christmas

Christmas traditions in the 1930s were not the same as now. In the 1930s not all families exchanged Christmas presents and not all families had Christmas trees. As the children got older and they saw others getting presents and they insisted that they too give and receive present.[73] Christmas trees were a German tradition that was introduced to Lithuania after WWI.[74] Thus Christmas trees were not part of the Christmas tradition to second-generation Lithuanians whose parents had arrived between 1890 and the start of WWI. Again, seeing others celebrating with trees and decorations the children began to require trees - and a new custom was born.

> The unique straw ornaments, typical of Lithuanian Christmas trees today, have an interesting origin. Josephine Daužvardis, the wife of Petras Daužvardis, Consul General of Lithuania in Chicago, was asked to decorate a Christmas tree with Lithuanian ornaments as part of an international "Christmas Around the World" tree exhibition at the Museum of Science and Industry in Chicago. Wanting to distinguish the Lithuanian tree

---

[73] Conversation with John Bakshis December, 2001
[74] Arizona Chapter of the Lithuanian American Community
   http://www.lithaz.org/arts/xmas.html

from all others she with the help of Sisters of St. Casimir came up with the idea to use ornaments made of straw.[75]

Lithuanian Tree   Soda Straw Ornaments
O'Hare International Airport

Straw Ornaments

---

[75] Arizona Chapter of the Lithuanian American Community
http://www.lithaz.org/arts/xmas.html

Straw Ornaments
Lithuanian Research and Studies Center - Chicago

Kūčios

The Christmas Eve meal is called Kūčios. The traditional meal consists of twelve, non-meat, dishes: herrings, beet soup with little ears, fish, sauerkraut salad, oatmeal pudding, whole wheat, Christmas Eve biscuit, dried fruit compote and fruit pudding were commonly featured.[76]

The Christmas meal also features Plokštelė, a thin wafer similar to a communion wafer. Depending on the region a family is from, plokštelė is also known as kalėdaitis, kaledine aplotkelė, plotkelė, paplotėlis, plokštainėlis or Dievo pyragai. Before the meal the head of the household offers a prayer, breaks off a piece of wafer and passes the wafer around the table. All break off pieces and share the wafer.

---

[76] Daužvardis, Josephine J. - Popular Lithuanian Recipes, 5th edition, Lithuanian Catholic Press, 1971

Menu
Christmas Eve Supper

Christmas Wafers
(Plotkeles)

Cranberry Pudding
(Spanguoliu Kisielius)

Beet Soup
(Barsciu Sriuba)
Milk

Baked Stuffed Fish
(Kepta Zuvis)

Saurkraut Salad
(Rauginti Kopustai)

Marinated Herring
(Silkes)

Boiled Potatoes
(Virtos Bulves)

Mushroom Dumplings
(Grybu Virtiniai)

Christmas Biscuits
with Poppy Seed

(Zlizikai su Aguomu
Pienu)

Rye Bread
(Rugine Duona)

Christmas Bread
(Kaledu Pyragas)

The feast of Christmas is always preceded by four weeks of Advent, a period of "fasting and contemplation." "Kucios", Christmas Eve, is the last day of fasting, followed by sumptuous feasting.

No less than 12 dishes must be served at this special Christmas Eve meal, beginning with the recitation of Grace and the breaking of a special unleavened wafer, called "Plotkele". This wafer, blessed by the parish priest, is shared by all at the table, signifying a spirit of unity.[77]

Twelve Christmas Eve Dishes[78]

---

[77] Sisters of St. Casimir Auxiliary, Jubilee Jems, General Publishing and Binding, Iowa Falls, IA. 1971   page 192

[78] Photo by Elena Skalisius

Easter

Egg decoration

Easter Eggs are highly decorated eggs. The designs are range from simple to very complex. There are three techniques used to decorate the eggs.

The scratch-carve technique requires soaking onion skins in water overnight. The water skins are then removed and the eggs are boiled in the water. The eggs take on a brown color. The longer they are boiled, the darker the color. The eggs are removed from the water and cooled. A design is then etched into the shell using a sharp point such as a razor or knife.

The wax-resist technique begins with placing a boiled egg into a pale egg dye. The egg is allowed to dry, and then bee's wax is applied in a pattern that protects the color beneath. The egg is then placed in a slightly darker dye. Subsequent layers are applied to complete the pattern. The bee's wax is then heated and removed to reveal the completed multi-colored design.

When eggs are completed a coating of clear fingernail polish can be applied. The coating will preserve the egg indefinitely. Over time the egg yolk and egg white will dry out. There is no odor unless the shell is broken.

Lithuanian Easter eggs (Margučiai) decorated by Zunė Zilevičienė
Displayed at the Lithuanian Museum of Art, Lemont, Illinois
collection of the artist (photo by R. Vaitkus)

Ethnic Easter 1974

The coloring and decorating of Easter eggs is a challenge to everyone's artistic ability. Colored eggs are a must at the Easter breakfast.

Egg Tapping Game

A favorite game among the kids was a contest to see who had the hardest egg. The contestants would tap two eggs together until a shell cracked and was 'captured'. The strategy here was to tap with the strong pointed tip of the egg and hope that your opponent used a different surface. You would also want to avoid being suckered into as many preliminary tapings as possible so that your egg wouldn't develop structural fatigue.

Egg Rolling Game

Another version of the egg-tapping game was the Egg Rolling Game. Everyone had several eggs. Contestants take turns rolling eggs down a ramp trying to tap each other's eggs. That is the eggs were aimed and then released, not pushed, down the ramp. Because of the irregular shape of the eggs they will hook left or right depending on the point. The trick was to compensate for the hook prior to release. When you tapped an egg it was 'captured', and you could pick it up and add it to your cache. The person with the most eggs (or all of the eggs) at the end of the contest was the winner.

Noah, Sarah and Bob Bakshis
Egg Rolling Game

Easter Table
(Velyku Stalas)

Colored Hard Boiled Eggs
(Margučiai)

Homemade Horseradish
(Krenai)

Stuffed Roasted Goose or Duck (Dešros)
(Žąsis Idaryta)

Easter Butter Lamb
(Avinelis)

Crullers
(Gruždai)

Homemade Cheese
(Sūris)

Fruit

Cold Baked Ham
 (Kumpis)

Homemade Sausage

Vegetable Salad

(Vinagretas)

Easter Bread
(Boba)

Sour Cream Butter

Coffee
(Kava)

The menu for Easter listed on this page was served throughout the holiday season. The festivities for this Christian holiday lasted for approximately one week.   The   season   would   end   with   LOW SUNDAY, affectionately referred to in some areas as "Little Easter."[79]

---

[79] Sisters of St. Casimir Auxiliary, Jubilee Jems, General Publishing and
   Binding, Iowa Falls, IA. 1971   page 193

Conclusion

The Lithuanian community of Waukegan and Lake County has been evolving for over 125 years. When Domininkas Norkevičia-Norkus arrived in 1891 he was the only Lithuanian in Waukegan. Norkus had to adjust to a culture that was dramatically different than that of his homeland. He would face the challenges of learning new a language and the demands of an industrialized society. Literally he faced the challenge of becoming an American.

As additional Lithuanian immigrants arrived a vibrant community was built around St. Bartholomew Church and the Lithuanian Hall, both of which supported social life. Choirs, theater groups, dances, and parties were all part of the community's social life.

Reflective of societies in general the process of assimilation begins when one culture meets another and the two blend. As time passes adherence to native customs erode and new customs take their place or old customs adjust to their new environment. The use of a native language may continue at home, but the language of the host society becomes increasingly dominant. Some elements of Lithuanian customs may persevere for generations. The most public element of being a Lithuanian or of Lithuanian descent is the surname. Through the immigration process obvious "Lithuanian" names have been corrupted or anglicized. For example, major league baseball player John Dickus became Johnny Dickshot; and basketball star Vytautas Budriūnas became Walter Budrun. The parents of WWII casualty Raymond Bujan used the surname Bujanauskas. Also, finding multiple alternative spellings for a family's surname is not uncommon. For example, the Lithuanian surname Bakšys has been alternatively spelled Bachis, Bakzhis and Bakshis on various government documents.

Demographic changes have moved the Lithuanian community from the south end of Waukegan to one that is dispersed throughout Waukegan, Lake, McHenry, and northern Cook County. Social activities that were once focused around St. Bartholomew Church are now organized by the Lithuanian American Community of Waukegan-Lake County. The community still celebrates Lithuanian independence in February and also celebrates Lithuanian customs in late summer near the anniversary of St. Bartholomew. The Waukegan-Lake County Lithuanian American Community has programs to teach Lithuanian customs and traditions to the young people of the community.

The group faces challenges in keeping young people interested in their heritage and in getting descendants of the original families to become active in the group. Some efforts in that direction are being considered. The extent to which these efforts are successful will determine if the Waukegan-Lake County Lithuanian American Community's celebration of their heritage extends beyond the life-span of the newest wave of immigrants.

One challenge faced by the Lithuanian American community is how to appeal to descendants of previous immigrants. With each successive generation there is a greater likelihood of marriage to a non-Lithuanian. The grandchildren or great-grandchildren of an immigrant often become what are called hyphenated American. That is their ethnicity is describes in fractional terms. These fractions could easily become complex. A grandchild could be half Polish and half Lithuanian; or half Slovenian and half Lithuanian; or even one-quarter Dutch, one-eighth German, one-eighth English, and one-half Lithuanian. Parents were faced with being upset because their children were getting married to non-Lithuanians, or being happy because their spouses were probably Catholic. These children from these marriages may claim to be Lithuanian by virtue of their names or their contact with a Lithuanian parent or grandparent. But they could also simultaneously claim to be Polish, Slovenian, Dutch, German or English.

Dilution of "Lithuanian stock" theoretically could happen very quickly. Assume that the original immigrant (first-generation) married a non-Lithuanian and successive generations continued to do the same. The percentage of "Lithuanian stock" in succeeding generations would be as follows:

Generation	Percent Lithuanian
First	100%
Second	50%
Third	25%
Fourth	12.5%
Fifth	6.25%
Sixth	3.13%
Seventh	1.56%

The Waukegan-Lake County Lithuanian community has existed for over 125 years. That is equivalent to about six generations. Thus, the descendants of the original founders of the community could range from being 100% Lithuanian to potentially as little as 3.13% Lithuanian. If the descendants were all male the family name would have been passed down through the generations and the family could be easily identified as being of Lithuanian origin. If, however, any descendant were female, then naming customs would soon lose the Lithuanian surname, and the identity of "Lithuanian" would become either lost or a distant memory.

Descendant's identification as being "Lithuanian" may also not be reciprocated by first-generation Lithuanians.

> In America my sister she asked me "How do you call grandchildren?" I call them Americans. My daughter married a Slovenian. I call them Americans. If the father was born here and parents were Lithuanian but mothers are not - they are American. My kids are full-blooded Lithuania, because father and I are Lithuanians. But their kids no – they are mixed. They get married again - again mixed marriages, so that is American.[80]

The influence of the first immigrants dominated social activities of the community for over 70 years. The influence of displaced persons started in 1948 and continues now nearly 70 years later. Recent post-liberation immigrants have contributed to the community for almost 30 years. The three groups all had similar intents: to build a better life for themselves and their children, and to preserve the traditions of their homeland. Each group has

---

[80] Robert Bakshis, Conversation with Anna Chapas and Anna Bakshis November 29, 1975

had unique motivations for coming to American, and each group has attempted to preserve elements of Lithuanian culture in its own way.

The earliest immigrants were fleeing economic hardship and came to America to find jobs in the coal mines of and new industries of the Northeast and Midwest. Since most were farmers in Lithuanian and the new jobs were in industry they had to learn a new way of life and a new language. Immigration was open to Lithuanians from 1890 until WWI brought a stop to migration. Following WWI <u>The Emergency Quota Act of 1921</u> and <u>The Immigration Act of 1924</u> all but cut off immigration from Lithuania. Organizations such as the Lovers of Liberty worked for the establishment of a free and independent Lithuania which came about in 1918. They continued to support Lithuanian freedom even after Lithuania was absorbed by the Soviet Union during WWII.

The second wave's immigrants were the displaced persons from WWII. They had been removed from their homes in Lithuania during the war, and then they were not allowed to return after the war. This group included both farmers and professionals. Many in this group would have preferred to have returned to their homes in Lithuanian, but that was not possible because of political changes in Lithuania. The establishment of a Lithuania free from Soviet rule was a major concern for this group. They worked tirelessly until success was achieved in 1990 when Lithuania was again free from Russian rule. Their activities were coordinated by the Lithuanian American Community, Inc.

The third wave of immigrants came following the re-establishment of Lithuanian independence in 1990. Citizens of Lithuania were able to freely leave the country. Opportunities to relocate in the United States were open to professionals and educated individuals. This group has actively participated in the LAC to advance progress in their native Lithuania and perpetuate Lithuanian culture among their descendants.

Whether a person is was born in Lithuanian or is the descendent of a first-wave Lithuanian; whether they are 100% first-generation Lithuanian or 1.5% seventh-generation Lithuanian, they can all say: "Mes Lietuviai - We are Lithuanian."

Contributors

A special Ačiū Labai (Thank you very much) to the many people who assisted in identifying and locating people, events and materials that needed to be included in this history:

Charles Bagdon, John and Eva Bakshis, Balzekas Museum of Lithuanian Culture, Roseanne Ditzig, Meg Romero Hall (Director of Archives and Records Center - Archdiocese of Chicago), Dan Gust, Fr. Bart Juncer, Kaius Kaselionis, Beverly Millard (Waukegan Historical Society), Loretta Motiaytis-Hegel, Fr. Mike Nacius, Fr. Brian Paulson, S.J., Ty Rohrer (Waukegan Historical Society), Violeta Rutkauskienė, Richard Shaulis, Elena Skalisius (Lithuanian American Community of Waukegan-Lake County), Gintautas Steponavičius (President, Lithuanian American Community of Waukegan-Lake County), Vesta Steponavičiūtė (Lithuanian American Community of Waukegan-Lake County), Loreta Timukienė (Lithuanian Research and Studies Center), Palmira Petrauskas-Janusonis-Westholm (Lithuanian American Community of Waukegan-Lake County), Fr. Bill Zavaski (Last pastor of St. Bartholomew Church), Sr. Margaret Zalot (Sisters of St. Casimir), and Mary Novak-Zupec.

At the beginning of the new millennium the Waukegan-Lake County Lithuanian community received two unexpected and extremely gracious donations.

The Lithuanian American Community of Waukegan-Lake County, Inc. would like to acknowledge the generous support for their programs and activities provided by Algird Mickevicius and Birute Baltrus.

Algird Mickevicius passed away June 20, 2000 at the age of 85. He was a former chemical analyst for Proctor and Gamble and a member of the Board of the Lithuanian National Cemetery. According to his will the Lithuanian community received a generous endowment.

Then in April 2013, with great gratitude to Birute Baltrus, the Waukegan-Lake County Lithuanian community received the most generous endowment in the history of the community.

Birute Baltrus

In 2018 Birute Baltrus celebrated her 90th birthday. The Waukegan-Lake County Lithuanian American Community would like to wish her 100 more.

With much gratitude and appreciation the Waukegan-Lake County Lithuanian Community thanks both of you.

About the Author

Dr. Bakshis is a third-generation Lithuanian-American. His grandfather John Bakshis (Jonas Bakšys) came to Waukegan from Vidukle, Lithuania in 1912. He joined his brothers Frank, Anthony, Joseph, and James who had come to American earlier. Dr. Bakshis' grandmother Sophie Trusk (Sophie Truskauskaitė) arrived in Waukegan from Kulke, Lithuania a year later. They were married at St. Bartholomew Church October 8, 1917. John, Sophie and John's brother James opened Bakshis Brothers Grocery and Meat Market at 1002 8th Street a few years later. They had three children, 12 Grandchildren, 15 Great Grandchildren and numerous Great-Great Grandchildren,

Dr. Bakshis holds a Bachelor's degree in Mathematics and a Doctorate in Education from Northern Illinois University. He also has a Master's degree in Sociology from Illinois State University.

Dr. Bakshis has taught sociology at Illinois State University, Illinois Central Community College, and College of DuPage. He has served as an organizational researcher for College of DuPage, Triton College, World Book Educational Products, and Information Resources, Inc. He has also been a survey research consultant to various governmental groups. In addition, he has worked as a passenger Supervisor for the Transportation Security Administration at O'Hare International Airport. This service allowed him to meet Lithuanian-American U.S. Senator Dick Durbin and former Lithuanian President Valdas Adamkus and his wife Alma Adamkienė.

Dr. Bakshis and his wife, Maureen, live in Woodridge, IL. They have one son and three grandchildren.

Robert Bakshis

Notes